M. Xavier

Picciola

The Prisoner of Finestrella

M. Xavier

Picciola

The Prisoner of Finestrella

ISBN/EAN: 9783744759311

Printed in Europe, USA, Canada, Australia, Japan

Cover: Foto ©ninafisch / pixelio.de

More available books at **www.hansebooks.com**

PICCIOLA.

THE
PRISONER OF FINESTRELLA:
OR,
CAPTIVITY CAPTIVE.

BY X. B. SAINTINE.

A NEW EDITION, WITH ILLUSTRATIONS.

NEW YORK:
PHINNEY, BLAKEMAN & MASON,
61 WALKER STREET.
1861.

PUBLISHERS' ADVERTISEMENT.

During the eight years which have elapsed since the first appearance of PICCIOLA, it has assumed the position of a classic. It has been crowned by the Académie Française; and has passed through numberless editions, in every form, and at every price, from the costly and elegant *édition de luxe*, to the cheap volume for schools. It has been translated into several foreign languages. In England it has met with a cordial reception; and in this country, the favour with which it has been received is attested by the number of editions through which it has passed, the appearance of an impression in the original, and the demand for imported copies.

Under these circumstances, the publishers have thought that the numerous admirers of this beautiful little tale might be pleased to possess it in a form more suited to its merits than any in which it has heretofore appeared in this country; they have therefore prepared this edition, with Illustrations, and an Introduction from the author, with the assurance of an extended sale.

INTRODUCTORY EPISTLE

TO

MADAME VIRGINIE ANCELOT.

I HAVE re-read my book, and I tremble in offering it to you; yet who can appreciate it better? You like neither romances nor dramas; my work is neither a romance nor a drama.

The tale which I have related, madam, is simple; so simple, indeed, that perhaps never has pen laboured on a subject more utterly restricted. My heroine is so unimportant! Not that I wish beforehand to throw the fault of failure on her; for if the action of my little history is thus meagre, its principle is lofty, its aim is elevated; and if I fail in attaining my purpose, it will be that my strength is insufficient. Yet I am not careless as to the fate of my labor, for in it are the deepest of my convictions; and believe me that, more from benevolence than vanity, I hope, though the crowd of ordinary readers may pass over my work with carelessness, that still for some it may possess a charm, for others, utility.

Do you find interest in the truth of a story? If so, I offer that to you to compensate for what you may not find in the story itself.

You remember that lovely woman, so lately dead, the Countess de Charney, whose expression, though mournful, seemed already to breathe of Heaven. Her look, so open, so sweet, which seemed to caress while wandering over you, and to make the heart swell as it lingered; from which one turned away only to be drawn again within its enchantment; you have seen it, at first timid as that of a young girl, suddenly become animated, brilliant, and self-possessed, exhibiting all its native energy, power, and devotion. Such was the woman; a marvellous union of tenderness and courage, of the weakness of sense and the strength of soul.

Such have I known her; such did others know her, long before me, when her soul was excited only by the affections of a daughter and of a wife. You understand the pleasure with which I dwell with you on such a woman; I may not often again have the opportunity. Still, she is not the heroine of my story.

In the only visit which you made her at Belleville, where was the tomb of her husband, and now, alas! her own, you more than once seemed surprised with what you saw. You were struck with an old, white-haired man, who sat next her at table, whose appearance and manners were coarse, even for his class. You saw him speak familiarly with the daughter of the countess, who, beautiful as her mother had been, answered him with kindness, and even with deference, giving him the name of godfather, which, indeed, was the relation he bore to her. Perhaps you have not forgotten a flower, dried and colorless, in a rich case; and, also, that when you asked her concerning it, a saddened look stole over the countenance of the widow, and your questions remained unanswered. This answer you now have before you.

Honored with the confidence and affection of the countess, more than once, before that simple flower, between her and the venerable man, have I listened to long and touching details. Besides this, I hold the manuscripts of the count, his letters, and his two prison journals.

I have carefully retained in my memory those precious details; I have attentively perused those manuscripts; I have made important extracts from those letters; and in those journals have I found my inspiration. If, then, I succeed in rousing in your soul the feelings which have agitated mine in presence of these relics of the captive, my fears for my little book are vain.

One word. I have given throughout to my hero his title of count, even during a time in which such dignities were obsolete. This is because I have always heard him so called, in French and in Italian; and in my memory his name and his title are inseparably connected.

You now understand me, madam. You will not expect in this book a history of important events, or the vivid details of love. I have spoken of utility; and of what use is a love-story? In that sweet study, practice is worth more than theory, and each one needs his own experience: each one hastens to acquire it, and cares little to seek it already prepared in books. It is useless for old men, moralists by necessity, to cry, "Shun that dangerous rock, where we have once been shipwrecked!" Their children answer them, "You have tempted that sea, and we must tempt it in turn. We claim our right of shipwreck."

Yet is there in my story something still of love; but, before all, of a man's love for —— shall I tell you? No, read and you will learn.

X. B. SAINTINE.

PICCIOLA.

BOOK I.

CHAPTER I.

CHARLES VERAMONT, Count de Charney, whose name is not wholly effaced from the annals of modern science, and may be found inscribed in the mysterious archives of the police under Napoleon, was endowed by nature with an uncommon capacity for study. Unluckily, however, his intelligence of mind, schooled by the forms of a college education, had taken a disputatious turn. He was an able logician rather than a sound reasoner; and there was in Charney the composition of a learned man, but not of a philosopher.

At twenty-five, the count was master of seven languages; but instead of following the example of certain learned Polyglots, who seem to acquire foreign idioms for the express purpose of exposing their incapacity to the contempt of foreigners, as well as of their own countrymen, through a confusion of tongues, as well as intellect, Charney regarded his acquirements as a linguist only as a stepping-stone to others of higher value. Commanding the services of so many menials of the intellect, he assigned to each his business, his duty, his fields to cultivate. The Germans served him for metaphysics; the English and Italians for politics and jurisprudence; *all* for history; to the remotest sources of which he travelled in company with the Romans, Greeks, and Hebrews.

In devoting himself to these serious studies, the count did not neglect the accessory sciences. Till at length, alarmed by the extent of the vast horizon, which seemed to expand as he advanced; finding himself stumble at every step in the labyrinth in which he was bewildered—weary of the pursuit of Truth—(the unknown goddess,)—he began to contemplate history as the lie of ages, and attempted to reconstruct the edifice on a surer foundation. He composed a new historical romance, which the learned derided from envy, and society from ignorance.

Political and legislative science furnished him with more positive groundwork; but these, from one end of Europe to the other, were crying aloud for Reform; and when he tried to specify a few of the more flagrant abuses, they proved so deeply rooted in the social system,—so many destinies were based on a fallacious principle, that he was actually discouraged. Charney had not the strength of mind, or insensibility of heart, indispensable to overthrow, in other nations, all that the tornado of the Revolution had left standing in his own.

He recollected, too, that hosts of estimable men, as learned, and perhaps as well-intentioned as himself, professed theories in total opposition to his own. If he were to set the four quarters of the globe on fire for the mere satisfaction of a chimera? This consideration, more startling than even his historical doubts, reduced him to the most painful perplexity.

Metaphysics afforded him a last resource. In the ideal world, an overthrow is less alarming; since ideas may clash without danger in infinite space. In waging such a war, he no longer risked the safety of others; he endangered only his own peace of mind.

The farther he advanced into the mysteries of metaphysical science, analyzing, arguing, disputing,—the more deeply he became enveloped in darkness and mystery. Truth, ever flying from his grasp, vanishing under his gaze, seemed to deride him like the mockery of a will-o'-the-wisp, shining to delude the unwary. When he paused to admire its luminous brilliancy, all suddenly grew dark; the meteor having disappeared to shine again on some remote and unexpected point; and when, persevering and tenacious, Charney armed himself with patience, followed with steady steps, and attained the sanctuary, the fugitive was gone again! This time he had overstepped the mark! When he fancied the meteor was in his hand — grasped firmly in his hand — it had already slipped through his fingers, multiplying into a thousand brilliant and delusive particles. Twenty rival truths perplexed the horizon of his mind, like so many false beacons beguiling him to shipwreck. After vacillating between Bossuet and Spinoza,—deism and atheism,—bewildered among spiritualists, materialists, idealists, ontologists, and eclectics, he took refuge in universal scepticism, comforting his uneasy ignorance by bold and universal negation.

Having set aside the doctrine of innate ideas, and the revelation of theologians, as well as the opinions of Leibnitz, Locke, and Kant, the Count de Charney now resigned himself to the grossest pantheism, unscrupulously denying the existence of one high and supreme GOD. The contradiction existing between ideas and things, the irregularities of the created world, the unequal distribution of strength and endowment among mankind, inspired his overtasked brain with the conclusion that the world is a conglomeration of insensate matter, and CHANCE the lord of all.

Chance, therefore, became his GOD here, and nothingness his hope hereafter. He adopted his new creed with avidity—almost with triumph—as if the audacious invention had been his own. It was a relief to get rid of the doubts which tormented him by a sweeping clause of incredulity; and from that moment, Charney, bidding adieu to science, devoted himself exclusively to the pleasures of the world.

The death of a relation placed him in possession of a considerable fortune. France, reorganized by the consulate, was resuming its former habits of luxury and splendour. The clarion of victory was audible from every quarter; and all was joy and festivity in the capital. The Count de Charney figured brilliantly in the world of magnificence, elegance, taste, and enlightenment. Having attracted around him the gay, the graceful, and the witty, he unclosed the gates of his splendid mansion to the glittering divinities of the day,—to fashion, bon ton, and distinction of every kind. Lost in the giddy crowd, he took part in all its enjoyments and dissipations; amazed that amid such a vortex of pleasures he should still remain a stranger to happiness!

Music, dress, the perfumed atmosphere surrounding the fair and fashionable, were the chief objects of his interest. Vainly had he attempted to devote himself to the society of men renowned for wit and understanding. The ignorance of the learned, the errors of the wise, excited only his compassion or contempt.

Such is the misfortune of proficiency! No one reaches the artificial standard we have created. Even those who are as learned as ourselves are learned after some other fashion; and from our lofty eminence we look down upon mankind as upon a crowd of dwarfs and pigmies. In the hierarchy of intellect, as in that of power, elevation is isolated:—to be alone is the destiny of the great.

Vainly did the Count de Charney devote himself to sensual pleasures. In the infancy of a social system so long estranged from the joys of life, and still defiled by the blood-stained orgies of the Revolution, attired in rags and tatters of Roman virtue, yet emulating the licentious excesses of the regency, he signalized himself by his prodigality and dissipation. Labour lost.—Horses, equipages, a splendid table, balls, concerts, and hunting-parties, failed to secure Pleasure as his guest. He had friends to flatter him, mistresses to amuse his leisure; yet, though all these were purchased at the highest price, the count found himself as far as ever from the joys of love or friendship. Nothing availed to smooth the wrinkles of his heart, or force it into a smile: Charney actually *laboured* to be entrapped by the baits of society, without achieving captivation. The syren Pleasure, raising her fair form and enchanting voice above the surface of the waters, fascinated *the man*, but the eye of the philosopher could not refrain from plunging into the glassy depths below, to be disgusted by the scaly body and bifurcal tail of the ensnaring monster.

Truth and error were equally against him. To virtue he was a stranger, to vice indifferent. He had experienced the vanity of knowledge; but the bliss of ignorance was denied him. The gates of Eden were closed against his re-entrance. Reason appeared fallacious, joy apocryphal. The noise of entertainments wearied him; the silence of home was still more tedious; in company, he became a burden to others; in retirement, to himself. A profound sadness took possession of his soul!

In spite of all Charney's efforts, the demon of philosophical analysis, far from being exorcised, served to tarnish, undermine, contract, and extinguish the brilliancy of every mode of life he selected. The praise of his friends, the endearments of his loves, seemed nothing more than the current coin given in exchange for a certain portion of his property, the paltry evidence of a necessity for living at his expense.

Decomposing every passion and sentiment, and reducing all things to their primitive elements, he, at length, contracted a morbid frame of mind, amounting almost to aberration of intellect. He fancied that in the finest tissue composing his garments, he could detect the exhalations of the animal of whose fleece it was woven—on the silk of his gorgeous hangings, the crawling worm which furnishes them. His furniture, carpets, gewgaws, trinkets of coral or mother-of-pearl, all were stigmatized in his eyes as the spoil of the dead, shaped by the labours of some squalid artisan. The spirit of inquiry had destroyed every illusion. The imagination of the sceptic was paralyzed!

To such a heart as that of Charney, however, emotion was indispensable. The love which found no single object on which to concentrate its vigour expanded into tenderness for all mankind; and he became a philanthropist!

With the view of serving the cause of his fellow-creatures, he devoted himself to politics, no longer speculative, but active; initiated himself into secret societies, and grew a fanatic for freedom, the only superstition remaining for those who have renounced the higher aspirations of human nature. He enrolled himself in a plot!—a conspiracy against nothing less than the sovereignty of the victorious Napoleon!

In this attempt, Charney fancied himself actuated by patriotism, by philanthropy, by love of his countrymen!—More likely by animosity against the one great man, of whose power and glory he was envious! An aristocrat at heart, he fancied himself a leveller. The proud noble who had been robbed of the title of count, bequeathed him by his ancestors, did not choose that his inferior in birth should assume the title of emperor, which he had conquered at the point of his sword.

It matters little in what plot he embarked his destinies; at that epoch, there was no lack of conspiracies! It was one of the many hatched between 1803 and 1804, and not suffered to come to light: the police—that second providence which presides over the safety of empires—was beforehand with it! Government decided that the less noise made on the occasion, the better; they would not even spare it so much as a discharge of muskets on the Plaine de Grenelle, the scene of military execution: but the heads of the conspiracy were privately arrested, condemned, almost without trial, and conveyed away to solitary confinement in various state prisons, citadels, or fortresses, of the ninety-six departments of consular France.

CHAPTER II.

In traversing the Alps on my way to Italy,—an humble tourist, with my staff in my hand, and my wallet on my shoulder, I remember pausing to contemplate, near the pass of Rodoretto, a torrent swollen by the melting of the glaciers. The tumultuous sounds produced by its course, the foaming cascades into which it burst, the varying colours and hues created by the movement of its waters, yellow, white, green, black, according to its channel through marl, slate, chalk, or peat earth,—the vast blocks of marble or granite it had detached without being able to remove, around which a thousand ever-changing cataracts added roar to roar, cascade to cascade; the trunks of trees it had uprooted, of which the still foliaged branches emerging from the water were agitated by the winds, while the roots were buffeted by the waves; fragments of the very banks clothed with verdure, and driven like floating islands against the trees, as the trees were driven in their turn against the blocks of granite;—all this, these murmurs, clashings, and roarings, confined between narrow and precipitous banks, impressed me with wonder and admiration. And this torrent was the Clusone!

Skirting its shores, I pursued the course of the stream into one of the four valleys retaining the name of "Protestant," in the memory of the Vaudois who formerly took refuge in their solitudes.

There, my torrent lost its wild irregularity; and its hundred roaring voices were presently subdued. Its shattered trees and islands had been deposited on some adjacent level; its colours had resolved themselves into one; and the material of its bed no longer distinguishable on the tranquil surface. Still strong and copious, it now flowed with decency, propriety, almost with coquetry: affecting the airs of a modest rivulet as it bathed the rugged walls of Fenestrella.

It was then I visited Fenestrella, a large town celebrated for peppermint water, and the fortress which crowns the two mountains between which it is situated, communicating with each other by covered ways, but partly dismantled during the wars of the Republic. One of the forts, however, was repaired and refortified when Piedmont became incorporated into France.

In this fortress of Fenestrella, was Charles Veramont, Count de Charney, incarcerated, on an accusation of having attempted to subvert the laws of government, and introduce anarchy and confusion into the country.

Estranged by rigid imprisonment, alike from men of science and men of pleasure, and regretting neither,—renouncing without much effort his wild projects of political regeneration,—bidding a forced farewell to his fortune, by the pomps of which he had been undazzled,—to his friends, who were grown tiresome, and his mistresses, who were grown faithless; having for his abode, instead of a princely mansion, a bare and gloomy chamber;—the gaoler of Charney was now his sole attendant, and his imbittered spirit his only companion.

But what signified the gloom and nakedness of his apartment? The necessaries of life were there, and he had long been disgusted with its superfluities.—Even his gaoler gave him no offence. It was only his own thoughts that troubled him!

Yet what other diversions remained for his solitude — but self-conference?—Alas! none! Nothing around him or before him but weariness and vexation of spirit! All correspondence was interdicted. He was allowed no books, nor pens, nor paper; for such was the established discipline at Fenestrella. A year before, when the count was intent only on emancipating himself from the perplexities of learning, this loss might have seemed a gain. But now, a book would have afforded a friend to consult, or an adversary to be confuted! Deprived of every thing, sequestered from the world, Charney had nothing left for it, but to become reconciled to himself, and live in peace with that natural enemy, his soul. For the cruelty with which that unsilenceable monitor continued to set before him the desperateness of his condition, rendered conciliation necessary. His case was indeed a hard one! A man to whom nature had been so prodigal, whose cradle society had surrounded with honours and privileges,—*he* to be reduced to such abject insignificance!—*he* to have need of pity and protection, who had faith neither in the existence of a God nor the mercy of his fellow-creatures!

Vainly did he strive to throw off this frightful consciousness, when in the solitude of his reveries it alternately chilled and scorched his shrinking bosom: and once more, the unhappy Charney began to cling for support to the visible and material world,— now, alas! how circumscribed around him. The room assigned to his use was at the rear of the citadel, in a small building raised upon the ruins of a vast and strong foundation, serving formerly for defence, but rendered useless by a new system of fortification.

Four walls, newly whitewashed, so that he was denied even the amusement of perusing the lucubrations of former prisoners, his predecessors; a table, serving for his meals; a chair, whose insulated unity reminded him, that no human being would ever sit beside him there in friendly converse; a trunk for his clothes and linen: a little sideboard of painted deal, half worm-eaten, offered a singular contrast to the rich mahogany dressing-case, inlaid with silver, standing there as the sole representative of his former splendours. A clean, but narrow bed, window-curtains of blue cloth (a mere mockery, for, thanks to the closeness of his prison bars and the opposite wall rising at ten feet distance, there was little to fear from prying eyes or the importunate radiance of the sun.) Such was the complement of furniture allotted to the Count de Charney.

Over his chamber was another, wholly unoccupied; he had not a single companion in that detached portion of the fortress.

The remainder of his world consisted in a short, massive, winding stone staircase, descending into a small paved court, sunk into what had been a moat, in the earlier days of the citadel, in which narrow space he was permitted to enjoy air and exercise during two hours of the day. Such was the ukase of the commandant of Fenestrella.

From this confined spot, however, the prisoner was able to extend his glance towards the summits of the mountains, and command a view of the vapours rising from the plain; for the walls of the ramparts, lowering suddenly at the extremity of the glacis, admitted a limited proportion of air and sunshine into the court. But once shut up again in his room, his view was bounded by an horizon of solid masonry, and a surmise of the majestic and picturesque aspect of nature it served to conceal. Charney was well aware that to the right rose the fertile hills of Saluces; that to his left were developed the last undulations of the valley of Aorta and the banks of the Chiara; that before him lay the noble plains of Turin; and behind, the mighty chain of Alps, with its adornment of rocks, forests, and chasms, from Mount Genevra to Mount Cenis. But, in spite of this charming vicinage, all he was permitted to behold was the misty sky suspended over his head by a framework of rude masonry; the pavement of the little court, and the bars of his prison, through which he might admire the opposite wall, adorned with a single small square window, at which he had once or twice caught glimpses of a doleful human countenance.

What a world from which to extract delight and entertainment! The unhappy Count wore out his patience in the attempt! At first, he amused himself with scribbling with a morsel of charcoal on the walls of his prison the dates of every happy event of his childhood; but from this dispiriting task he desisted, more discouraged than ever. The demon of scepticism next inspired him with evil counsel; and having framed into fearful sentences the axioms of his withering creed, he inscribed them also on his wall, between recollections consecrated to his sister and mother!

Still unconsoled, Charney at length made up his mind to fling aside his heart-eating cares, adopt, by anticipation, all the puerilities and brutalization which result from the prolongation of solitary confinement. The philosopher attempted to find amusement in unravelling silk or linen; in making flageolets of straw, and building ships of walnut-shells. The man of genius constructed whistles, boxes, and baskets, of kernels; chains and musical instruments, with the springs of his braces; nay, for a time, he took delight in these absurdities; then, with a sudden movement of disgust, trampled them, one by one, under his feet!

To vary his employment, Charney began to carve a thousand fanciful designs upon his wooden table! No schoolboy ever mutilated his desk by such attempts at arabesque, both in relief and intaglio, as tasked his patience and address. The celebrated portal of the church of Candebee, and the pulpit and palm trees of St. Gudula at Brussels, are not adorned with a greater variety of figures. There were houses upon houses, fishes upon trees, men taller than steeples, boats upon roofs, carriages upon water, dwarf pyramids, and flies of gigantic stature,— horizontal, vertical, oblique, topsy-turvy, upside down, pell-mell, a chaos of hieroglyphics, in which he tried to discover a sense symbolical, an accidental intention, an occult design; for it was no great effort on the part of one who had so much faith in the power of chance, to expect the developement of an epic poem in the sculptures on his table, or a design of Raphael in the veins of his box-wood snuff-box.

It was the delight of his ingenuity to multiply difficulties for conquest, problems for solution, enigmas for divination; but even in the midst of these recreations, ennui, the formidable enemy, again surprised the captive.

The man whose face he had noticed at the grated window, might have afforded him food for conjecture, had he not seemed to avoid the observation of the Count, by retiring the moment Charney made his appearance; in consequence of which, he conceived an abhorrence of the recluse. Such was his opinion of the human species, that the stranger's desire of concealment convinced him he was a spy, employed to watch the movements of the prisoners, or, perhaps, some former enemy, exulting over his humiliation.

On interrogating the gaoler, however, this last supposition was set at rest.

" 'Tis an Italian," said Ludovico, the turnkey. " A good soul,— and, what is more, a good Christian; for I often find him at his devotions."

Charney shrugged his shoulders: " And what may be the cause, pray, of his retention?" said he.

" He attempted to assassinate the Emperor."

"Is he, then, a patriot?"

"A patriot! Rubbish! Not he. But the poor soul had once a son and daughter: and *now* he has only a daughter. The son was killed in Germany. A cannon-ball broke a tooth for him. *Povero figliuolo!*"

"It was a paroxysm of selfishness, then, which moved this old man to become an assassin?"

"You have never been a father, *Signor Conte!*" replied the gaoler. "*Cristo Santo!* if my Antonio, who is still a babe, were to eat his first mouthful for the good of this empire of the French (which is a bantling of his own age, or thereabouts,) I'd soon —— But *basta!* I've no mind to take up my lodging at Fenestrella, except as it may be with the keys at my girdle or under my pillow."

"And how does this fierce conspirator amuse himself in prison?" persisted Charney.

"Catching flies!" replied the gaoler, with an ironical wink

Instead of detesting his brother in misfortune, Charney now began to despise him. "A madman, then?" he demanded.

"*Perche pazzo, Signor Conte?* Though you are the last comer, you excel him already in the art of hacking a table into devices. *Pazienza!*"

In defiance of the sneer conveyed in the gaoler's remark, Charney soon resumed his manual labours, and the interpretations of his hieroglyphics; but, alas! only to experience anew their insufficiency as a kill-time. His first winter had expired in weariness and discontent: when, by the mercy of Heaven, an unexpected object of interest was assigned him.

CHAPTER III.

ONE day, Charney was breathing the fresh air in the little court of the fortress, at the accustomed hour, his head declining, his eyes downcast, his arms crossed behind him, pacing with slow and measured steps, as if his deliberation tended to enlarge the precincts of his dominion.

Spring was breaking. A milder air breathing around, tantalized him with a vain inclination to enjoy the season of liberty, as master of his time and territory. He was proceeding to number, one by one, the stones paving the court-yard, (doubtless to verify the accuracy of former calculations,—for it was by no means the first time they had put his arithmetic to the test,) when he perceived a small mound of earth rising between two stones of the pavement, cleft slightly at its summit.

The Count stopped short—his heart beat hurriedly without any rational grounds for emotion, except that every trivial incident affords matter of hope or fear to a captive. In the most indifferent objects, in the most unimportant events, the prisoner discerns traces of a mysterious project for his deliverance.

Who could decide that this trifling irregularity on the surface might not indicate important operations under ground? Subterraneous issues might have been secretly constructed, and the earth be about to open and afford him egress towards the mountains! Perhaps his former friends and accomplices had been sapping and mining, to procure access to his dungeon, and restore him to light and liberty!

He listened! he fancied he could detect the low murmur of a subterraneous sound. He raised his head, and the loud and rapid clang of the tocsin saluted his ear. The ramparts were echoing with the prolonged roll of drums, like the call to arms in time of war. He started—he passed his trembling hand over his forehead, on which cold dews of intense agitation were already rising. Is his liberation at hand? Is France submitted to the domination of a new ruler?

The illusion of the captive vanished as it came. Reflection soon restored him to reason. He no longer possesses accomplices —he never possessed friends!—Again he lends a listening ear. and the same noises recur; but they mislead his mind no longer. The supposed tocsin is only the church bell which he has been accustomed to hear daily at the same hour, and the drums, the usual evening signal for retreat to quarters. With a bitter smile, Charney begins to compassionate his own folly, which could mistake the insignificant labours of some insect or reptile, some wandering mole or field-mouse, for the result of human fidelity, or the subversion of a mighty empire.

Resolved, however, to bring the matter to the test, Charney, bending over the little hillock, gently removed the earth from its summit; when he had the mortification to perceive that the wild though momentary emotion by which he had been overcome, was not produced by so much as the labours of an animal armed with teeth and claws! but by the efforts of a feeble plant to pierce the soil—a pale and sickly scatterling of vegetation. Deeply vexed, he was about to crush with his heel the miserable weed, when a refreshing breeze, laden with the sweets of some bower of honeysuckles, or syringas, swept past, as if to intercede for mercy towards the poor plant, which might perhaps hereafter reward him with its flowers and fragrance.

A new conjecture conspired to suspend his act of vengeance How has this tender plant, so soft and fragile as to be crushed with a touch, contrived to pierce and cleave asunder the earth, dried and hardened into a mass by the sun, daily trodden down by his own footsteps, and all but cemented by the flags of granite between which it was enclosed? On stooping again to examine the matter with more attention, he observed at the extremity of the plant a sort of fleshy valve affording protection to its first and tenderest leaves, from the injurious contact of any hard bodies they might have to encounter in penetrating the earthy crust in search of light and air.

" This, then, is the secret?" cried he, already interested in his discovery. " Nature has imparted strength to the vegetable germ, even as the unfledged bird which is able to break asunder with its beak the egg-shell in which it is imprisoned; happier than myself — in possession of unalienable instruments to secure its liberation!" And after gazing another minute on the inoffensive plant, he lost all inclination for its destruction.

On resuming his walk the next day, with wide and careless steps, Charney was on the point of setting his foot on it, from inadvertence; but luckily recoiled in time. Amused to find himself interested in the preservation of a weed, he paused to take note of its progress. The plant was strangely grown; and the free light of day had already effaced the pale and sickly complexion of the preceding day. Charney was struck by the power inherent in vegetables to absorb rays of light, and, fortified by the nourishment, borrow, as it were, from the prism, the very colours predestined to distinguish its various parts of organization.

" The leaves," thought he, " will probably imbibe a hue different from that of the stem. And the flowers? what colour, I wonder, will be the flowers? Nourished by the same sap as the green leaves and stem, how do they manage to acquire, from the influence of the sun, their variegations of azure, pink, or scarlet?— For already their hue is appointed. In spite of the confusion and disorder of all human affairs, matter, blind as it is, marches with admirable regularity: still blindly, however! for lo, the fleshy lobes which served to facilitate for the plant its progress through the soil, though now useless, are feeding their superfluous substance at its expense, and weighing upon its slender stalk!"

But, even as he spoke, daylight became obscured. A chilly spring evening, threatening a frosty night, was setting in; and the two lobes, gradually rising, seemed to reproach him with his objections, by the practical argument of enclosing the still tender foliage, which they secured from the attacks of insects or the inclemency of the weather, by the screen of their protecting wings.

The man of science was better able to comprehend this mute answer to his cavilling, because the external surface of the vegetable bivalve had been injured the preceding night by a snail, whose slimy trace was left upon the verdure of the cotyledon.

This curious colloquy between action and cogitation, between the plant and the philosopher, was not yet at an end. Charney was too full of metaphysical disquisition to allow himself to be vanquished by a good argument.

" 'Tis all very well!" cried he. " In this instance, as in others, a fortunate coincidence of circumstances has favoured the developement of incomplete creation. It was the inherent qualification of the nature of the plant to be born with a lever in order to upraise the earth, and a buckler to shelter its tender head: without which it must have perished in the germ, like myriads of individuals of its species which proved incapable of accomplishing their destinies. How can one guess the number of unsuccessful efforts which nature may have made, ere she perfected a single subject sufficiently organized! A blind man may sometimes shoot home; but how many uncounted arrows must be lost before he attains the mark? For millions of forgotten centuries, matter has been triturating between negative and positive attraction. How then can one wonder that chance should sometimes produce coincidence? This fleshy screen serves to shelter the early leaves. Granted! But will it enlarge its dimensions to contain the rest as they are put forth, and defend them from cold and insects? No, no; no evidence of the calculating of a presiding Providence! A lucky chance is the alpha and omega of the universe!"

Able logician!—profound reasoner! listen, and Nature shall find a thousand arguments to silence your presumption! Deign only to fix your inquiring eyes upon this feeble plant, which the munificence of Heaven has called into existence between the stones of your prison! You are so far right that the cotyledon will *not* expand so as to cover with its protecting wings the future progress of the plant. Already withering, they will eventually fall and decay. But they will suffice to accomplish the purpose of nature. So long as the northern wind drives down from the Alps their heavy fogs or sprinkling of sleet, the new leaves will find a retreat impermeable to the chilly air, caulked with resinous or viscous matter, and expanding or closing according to the impulse of the weather; finally distended by a propitious atmosphere, the leaflets will emerge clinging to each other for mutual support, clothed with a furry covering of down to secure them against the fatal influence of atmospheric changes. Did ever mother watch more tenderly over the preservation of a child? Such are the phenomena, Sir Count, which you might long ago have learned to admire, had you descended from the flighty regions of human science, to study the humble though majestic works of God! The deeper your researches, the more positive had been your conviction; for where dangers abound, know that the protection of the Providence which you deny is vouchsafed a thousand and a thousand fold in pity to the blindness of mankind!

In the weariness of captivity, Charney was soon satisfied to occupy his idle hours by directing his attention to the transformations of the plant. But when he attempted to contend with it in argument, the answers of the vegetable logician were too much for him.

"To what purpose these stiff bristles, disfiguring a slender stem?" demanded the Count. And the following morning he found them covered with rime: thanks to their defence, the tender bark had been secured from all contact with the frost.

"To what purpose, for the summer season, this winter garment of wool and down?" he again inquired. And when the summer season really breathed upon the plant, he found the new shoots array themselves in their light spring clothing; the downy vestments, now superfluous, being laid aside.

"Storms may be still impending!" cried Charney, with a bitter smile; "and how will these slender and flexile shoots resist the cutting hail, the driving wind?" But when the stormy rain arose, and the winds blew, the slender plant, yielding to their intemperance, replied to the sneers of the Count by prudent prostration. Against the hail, it fortified itself by a new manœuvre; the leaves, rapidly uprising, adhered to the stalks for protection; presenting to the attacks of the enemy the strong and prominent nerves of their inferior surface; and union, as usual, produced strength. Firmly closed together, they defied the pelting shower; and the plant remained master of the field; not, however, without having experienced wounds and contusions, which, as the leaves expanded in the returning sunshine, were speedily cicatrized by its congenial warmth.

"Is chance endowed then with intelligence?" cried Charney. "Must we admit matter to be spiritualized, or humiliate the world of intelligence into materialism?"

Still, though self-convicted, he could not refrain from interrogating his mute instructress. He delighted in watching, day by day, her spontaneous metamorphoses. Often, after having examined her progress, he found himself gradually absorbed in reveries of a more cheering nature than those to which he had been of late accustomed. He tried to prolong the softened mood of mind by loitering in the court beside the plant; and one day, while thus employed, he happened to raise his eyes towards the grated window, and saw the fly-catcher observing him. The colour rose to his cheek, as if the spy could penetrate the subject of his meditations; but a smile soon chased away the blush. He no longer presumed to despise his comrade in misfortune. *He*, too, had been engaged in contemplating one of the simplest creations of nature; and had derived comfort from the study.

"How do I know," argued Charney, "that the Italian may not have discovered as many marvels in a fly, as I in a nameless vegetable?"

The first object that saluted him on his returning to his chamber, after this admission, was the following sentence, inscribed by his own hand upon the wall, a few months before:—

"CHANCE, THOUGH BLIND, IS THE SOLE AUTHOR OF THE CREATION."

Seizing a piece of charcoal, Charney instantly qualified the assertion, by the addition of a single word—"Perhaps."

CHAPTER IV.

CHARNEY had long ceased to find amusement in these gratuitous mural inscriptions; and if he still occasionally played the sculptor with his wooden table, his efforts produced nothing now but germinating plants; each protected by a cotyledon, or a sprig of foliage, whose leaves were delicately serrated and prominently nerved. The greater portion of the time assigned him for exercise was spent in contemplation of his plant,—in examining and reasoning upon its developement. Even after his return to his chamber, he often watched the little solitary through his prison-bars. It had become his whim, his bauble, his hobby;—perhaps only to be discarded like other preceding favourites!

One morning, as he stood at the window, he observed the gaoler, who was rapidly traversing the court-yard, pass so close to it that the stem seemed on the point of being crushed under his footsteps; and Charney actually shuddered! When Ludovico arrived as usual with his breakfast, the Count longed to entreat the man would be careful in sparing the solitary ornament of his walk; but he found some difficulty in phrasing so puerile an entreaty. Perhaps the Fenestrella system of prison discipline might enforce the clearing of the court from weeds, or other vegetation. It might be a *favour* he was about to request, and the Count possessed no worldly means for the requital of a sacrifice. Ludovico had lady taxed him heavily, in the way of ransom, for the various objects with which it was his privilege to furnish the prisoners of the fortress.

Besides, he had scarcely yet exchanged a word with the fellow, by whose abrupt manners and character he was disgusted. His pride recoiled, too, from placing himself in the same rank with the fly-catcher, towards whom Ludovico had acknowledged his contempt. Then there was the chance of a refusal! The inferior, whose position raises him to temporary consequence, is seldom sufficiently master of himself to bear his faculties meekly, incapable of understanding that indulgence is a proof of power. The Count felt that it would be insupportable to him to find himself repulsed by a turnkey.

At length, after innumerable oratorical precautions, and the exercise of all his insight into the foibles of human nature, Charney commenced a discourse, logically preconcocted, in hopes to obtain his end without the sacrifice of his dignity,—or, to speak more correctly, of his pride.

He began by accosting the gaoler in Italian; by way of propitiating his natural prejudices, and calling up early associations. He inquired after Ludovico's boy, little Antonio; and, having caused this tender string to vibrate, took from his dressing-box a small gilt goblet, and charged him to present it to the child!

Ludovico declined the gift, but refused it with a smile; and Charney, though somewhat discountenanced, resolved to persevere. With adroit circumlocution, he observed, "I am aware tha a toy, a rattle, a *flower*, would be a present better suited to Antonio's age; but you can sell the goblet, and procure those trifles in abundance with the price." And, lo! *à propos of flowers*, the Count embarked at once into his subject.

Patriotism, paternal love, personal interest, every influential motive of human action, were thus put in motion in order to accomplish the preservation of a plant! Charney could scarcely have done more for his own. Judge whether it had ingratiated itself into his affections!

"*Signor Conte!*" replied Ludovico, at the conclusion of the harangue, "*riprendi sua nacchera indorata!* Were this pretty bauble missing from your toilet-case, its companions might fret after it! At three months old, my bantling has scarce wit enough to drink out of a goblet; and with respect to your gilly-flower—"

"*Is* it a gilly-flower?" inquired Charney, with eagerness.

"*Sac à papions!* how should I know? All flowers are more or less gilly-flowers! But as to sparing the life of yours, eccellenza, methinks the request comes late in the day. My boot would have

3*

been better acquainted with it long ago, had I not perceived your partiality for the poor weed!"

"Oh! as to my partiality," interrupted Charney, "I beg to assure you—"

"Ta, ta, ta, ta! What need of assurance," cried Ludovico. "I know whereabouts you are better than you do. Men *must* have *something* to love; and state prisoners have small choice allowed them in their whims. Why, among my boarders here, *Signor Conte*, (most of whom were grand gentry, and great wise-acres in their day, for 'tis not the small fry they send into harbour at Fenestrella,) you'd be surprised at what little cost they manage to divert themselves? One catches flies,—no harm in that; another—" and Ludovico winked knowingly, to signify the application—"another chops a solid deal table into chips, without considering how far I may be responsible for its preservation." The Count vainly tried to interpose a word: Ludovico went on: "some amuse themselves with rearing linnets and goldfinches; others have a fancy for white mice. For my part, poor souls, I have so much respect for their pets, that I had a fine Angora cat of my own, with long white silken hair, you'd have sworn 'twas a muff when 'twas asleep!—a cat that my wife doated on, to say nothing of myself. Well, I gave it away, lest the creature should take a fancy to some of their favourites. All the cats in the creation ought not to weigh against so much as a mouse belonging to a captive!"

"Well thought, well expressed, my worthy friend!" cried Charney, piqued at the inference which degraded him to the level of such wretched predilections. "But know that this plant is something more to me than a kill-time."

"What signifies? so it serves but to recall to your mind the green tree under which your mother hushed your infancy to rest, *per Bacco!* I give it leave to overshadow half the court. My instructions say nothing about weeding or hoeing, so e'en let it grow and welcome! Were it to turn out a tree, indeed, so as to assist you in escalading the walls, the case were different! But there is time before us to look after the business—eh! *eccellenza?*" said the gaoler, with a coarse laugh. "Not that you hav'n't my best wishes for the recovery of the free use of your legs and lungs; but all must come in course of time, and the regular way. For if you were to make an attempt at escape —"

"Well! and if I were?" said Charney, with a smile.

"Thunder and hail!—you'd find Ludovico a stout obstacle in your way! I'd order the sentry to fire at you, with as little scruple as at a rabbit! Such are my instructions! But as to doing mischief to a poor harmless gilly-flower, I look upon that man they tell of who killed the pet-spider of the prisoner under his charge, as a wretch not worthy to be a gaoler! 'Twas a base action, *eccellenza*,—nay, a crime!"

Charney felt amazed and touched by the discovery of so much sensibility on the part of his gaoler. But now that he had begun to entertain an esteem for the man, his vanity rendered it doubly essential to assign a rational motive for his passion.

" Accept my thanks, good Ludovico," said he, " for your goodwill. I own that the plant in question affords me scope for a variety of scientific observations. I am fond of studying its physiological phenomena." Then, (as Ludovico's vague nodding of the head convinced him that the poor fellow understood not a syllable he was saying,) he added, " more particularly as the class to which it belongs possesses medicinal qualities, highly favourable to a disorder to which I am subject."

A falsehood from the lips of the noble Count de Charney! and merely to evade the contempt of a gaoler, who, for the moment, represented the whole human species in the eyes of the captive.

"Indeed!" cried Ludovico; "then all I have to say is, that if the poor thing is so serviceable to you, you are not so grateful to it as you ought to be. If I hadn't been at the pains of watering it for you now and then, on my way hither with your meals, *la povera picciola* would have died of thirst. *Addio, Signor Conte!*"

"One moment, my good friend," exclaimed Charney, more and more amazed to discover such delicacy of mind so roughly enclosed, and repentant at having so long mistaken the character of his gaoler. "Since you have interested yourself in my pursuits, and without vaunting your services, accept, I entreat you, this small memento of my gratitude! Should better times await me, I will not forget you!"

And once more he tendered the goblet; which this time Ludovico examined with a sort of vague curiosity.

"Gratitude, for *what, Signor Conte?*" said he. "A plant wants nothing but a sprinkling of water; and one might furnish a whole parterre of them in their cups, without ruining oneself at the tavern. If *la picciola* diverts you from your cares, and provides you with a specific, enough said, and God speed her growth."

And having crossed the room, he quietly replaced the goblet in its compartment of the dressing-box.

Charney, rushing towards Ludovico, now offered him his hand.

"No, no!" exclaimed the gaoler, assuming an attitude of respect and constraint. "Hands are to be shaken only between equals and friends."

"Be my friend, then, Ludovico!" cried the Count.

"No, *eccellenza*, no!" replied the turnkey. "A gaoler must be on his guard, in order to perform his duties like a man of conscience, to-day, to-morrow, and every day of the week. If you were my friend, according to *my* notions of the word, how should I be able to call out to the sentinel, Fire! if I saw you swimming across the moat? I am fated to remain your keeper, gaoler, *e divotissimo servo!*"

CHAPTER V.

In the course of his solitary meditations, after Ludovico's departure, Charney was compelled to admit that, in his relations with the gaoler, the man of genius and education had fallen below the level of the man of the people. To what wretched subterfuges had he descended, in order to practise upon the feelings of this kind-hearted and simple being! He had even soiled his noble lips with an untruth.

He was startled to discover the services recently rendered by Ludovico to the "*povera picciola.*" The boor, the gaoler, morose only when invited to a breach of duty, had actually watched him in secret, not to exult over his weakness, but to render him a service; nay, by his obstinate disinterestedness, the man persisted in imposing an obligation on the Count de Charney.

In his walk next morning, the Count hastened to share, with his little favourite, the cruise of water allotted to his use; not only watering the roots, but sprinkling the plant itself, to refresh its leaves from dust or insects. While thus occupied, the sky became darkened by a thunder-cloud, suspended like a black dome over the turrets of the fortress. Large rain-drops began to fall: and Charney was about to take refuge in his room, when a few hailstones mingling with the rain, pattered down on the pavement of the court. La *povera picciola* seemed on the point of being uprooted by the whirlwind which accompanied the storm. Her dishevelled branches and leaves shrinking up towards their stalks for protection against the chilling shower, trembled with every driving blast of wind that howled, as if in triumph, through the court.

Charney paused. Recalling to mind the reproaches of Ludovico, he looked eagerly around for some object to defend his plant from the storm; but nothing could be seen. The hailstones came rattling down with redoubled force, threatening destruction to its tender stem; and, notwithstanding Charney's experience of its power of resistance against such attacks, he grew uneasy for its safety. With an effort of tenderness, worthy of a father or a lover, he stationed himself between his protegée and the wind, bending over her, to secure her from the hail; and, breathless with his struggles against the violence of the storm, devoted himself, like a martyr, to the defence of *la picciola.*

At length the hurricane subsided. But might not a recurrence of the mischief bring destruction to his favourite at some moment when bolts and bars divided her from her protector? He had already found cause to tremble for her safety, when the wife of Ludovico, accompanied by a huge mastiff, one of the guardians of the prison, occasionally traversed the yard; for a single stroke with its paw, or a snap of its mouth, might have annihilated the darling of the philosophical captive; and Charney accordingly passed the remainder of the day in concocting a plan of fortification.

The moderate portion of wood allowed him for fuel, scarcely supplied his wants in a climate whose nights and mornings are so chilly, in a chamber debarred from all warmth of sunshine. Yet he resolved to sacrifice his comfort to the safety of the plant. He promised himself to retire early to rest, and rise later; by which means, after a few days of self-denial, he amassed sufficient wood for his purpose.

"Glad to see you have more fuel than you require," cried Ludovico, on noticing the little stock. "Shall I clear the room for you of all this lumber?"

"Not for the world," replied Charney, with a smile. "I am hoarding it to build a palace for my lady-love."

The gaoler gave a knowing wink, which signified, however, that he understood not a word about the matter.

Meanwhile, Charney set about splitting and pointing the uprights of his bastions; and carefully laid aside the osier bands which served to tie up his daily fagots. He next tore from his trunk its lining of coarse cloth; out of which he drew the strongest threads: and his materials thus prepared, he commenced his operations the moment the rules of the prison and the exactitude of the gaoler would admit. He surrounded his plant with palisades of unequal height, carefully inserted between the stones of the pavement, and secured at the base by a cement of earth, laboriously collected from the interstices, and mortar and saltpetre secretly abstracted from the ancient turret-walls around him. When the labours of the carpenter and mason were achieved, he began to interlace his scaffolding at intervals with split osiers, to screen *la picciola* from the shock of exterior objects.

The completion of his work acquired, during its progress, new importance in his eyes, from the opposition of Ludovico. The gaoler shook his head and grumbled when first he noticed the undertaking. But before the close of the performance the kind-hearted fellow withdrew his disapprobation; nay, would even smoke his pipe, leaning against the wicket of the courtyard, and watching, with a smile, the efforts of the unpractised mechanic; interrupting himself in the enjoyment of his favourite recreation, however, to favour Charney with occasional counsels, the result of his own experience.

The work progressed rapidly; but, to render it perfect, the

Count was under the necessity of sacrificing a portion of his scanty bedding; purloining handfuls of straw from his palliasse, in order to band up the interstices of his basket-work, as a shelter against the mountain wind, and the fierceness of the meridian sun, which in summer would be reflected from the flint of the adjacent wall.

One evening, a sudden breeze arose, after Charney had been locked in for the night,—and the yard was quickly strewn with scattered straws and slips of osier, which had not been worked in with sufficient solidity. Charney promised himself to counteract next day the ill effects of his carelessness; but on reaching the court at the usual hour, he found that all the mischief had been neatly repaired: a hand more expert than his own had replaced the matting and palisades. It was not difficult to guess to whom he was indebted for this friendly interposition. Meanwhile, thanks to her friend,—*thanks to her friends*, the plant was now secured by solid ramparts and roofing: and Charney, attaching himself, according to the common frailty of human nature, more tenderly to the object on which he was conferring obligation, had the satisfaction to see the plant expand with redoubled powers, and acquire new beauties every hour. It was a matter of deep interest to observe the progress of its consolidation. The herbaceous stem was now acquiring ligneous consistency. A glossy bark began to surround the fragile stalk; and already, the gratified proprietor of this gratuitous treasure entertained eager hopes of the appearance of flowers among its leaves. The man of paralysed nerves,—the man of frost-bound feelings, had at length found something to wish for! The action of his lofty intellect was at last concentrated into adoration of an herb of the field. Even as the celebrated Quaker, John Bartram, resolved, after studying for hours the organization of a violet, to apply his powers of mind to the analysis of the vegetable kingdom, and eventually acquired high eminence among the masters of botanical science, Charney became a natural philosopher.

A learned pundit of Malabar is said to have lost his reason in attempting to expound the phenomena of the sensitive plant. But the Count de Charney seemed likely to be restored to the use of *his* by studies of a similar nature; and, sane or insane, he had at least already extracted from his plant an arcanum sufficiently potent to dispel the weariness of ennui, and enlarge the limit of his captivity.

"If it would but flower!"—he frequently exclaimed, "what a delight to hail the opening of its first blossom! a blossom whose beauty, whose fragrance, will be developed for the sole enjoyment of my eager senses. What will be its colour, I wonder! what the form of its petals?—time will show! Perhaps they may afford new premises for conjecture—new problems for solution. Perhaps the conceited gipsy will offer a new challenge to my understanding? So much the better! Let my little adversary arm herself with all her powers of argument. I will not prejudge the case. Perhaps, when thus complete, the secret of her mysterious nature will be apparent? How I long for the moment!—Bloom, picciola! bloom—and reveal yourself in all your beauty to him to whom you are indebted for the preservation of your life!"

"PICCIOLA!"—Such is the name, then, which, borrowed from the lips of Ludovico, Charney has involuntarily bestowed upon his favourite!—"Picciola!" *la povera picciola*, was the designation so tenderly appropriated by the gaoler to the *poor little thing* which Charney's neglect had almost allowed to perish.

"Picciola!" murmured the solitary captive, when every morning he carefully searched its already tufted foliage for indications of inflorescence; "when will these wayward flowers make their appearance!" The Count seemed to experience pleasure in the mere pronunciation of a name uniting in his mind the images of the two objects which peopled his solitude;—his gaoler and his plant!

Returning one morning to the accustomed spot, and, as usual, interrogating Picciola branch by branch, leaf by leaf, his eyes were suddenly attracted towards a shoot of unusual form, gracing the principal stem of the plant. He felt the beatings of his heart accelerated, and, ashamed of his weakness, the colour rose to his cheek, as he stooped for re-examination of the event. The spherical shape of the excrescence which presented itself, green, bristly, and imbricated with glossy scales, like the slates of a rounded dome surmounting an elegant kiosk, announced a bud!—Eureka! —A flower must be at hand!

CHAPTER VI.

THE fly-catcher, who occasionally made his appearance at his grated window, seemed to take delight in watching the assiduities of Charney towards his favourite! He had observed the Count compose his cement, weave his osier-work,—erect his palisades; and, admonished by his own long captivity of the moral influence of such pursuits, readily conjectured that a whole system of philosophy was developing itself in the mind of his fellow-prisoner.

One memorable day, a new face made its appearance at the window,—a female face,—fair, and fresh, and young. The stranger was a girl, whose demeanour appeared at once timid and lively;

modesty regulated the movements of her well-turned head, and the brilliancy of her animated eyes, whose glances were veiled by long silken eyelashes of raven darkness. As she stood behind the heavy grating, on which her fair hand bent for support, her brow inclining in the shade as if in a meditative mood, she might have stood for a chaste personification of the nymph Captivity. But when her brow was uplifted, and the joyous light of day fell on her lovely countenance, the harmony and serenity of her features, her delicate but brilliant complexion, proclaimed that it was in the free air of liberty she had been nurtured, not under the dispiriting influence of the bolts and bars of a dungeon. She was, perhaps, one of those tutelary angels of charity, whose lives are passed in soothing the sick and solacing the captive?—No!—the instinct which brought the fair stranger to Fenestrella was still more puissant,—even that of filial duty. Only daughter to Girardi the fly-catcher,—Teresa had abandoned the gay promenades and festivities of Turin, and the banks of the Doria-Riparia, to inhabit the cheerless town of Fenestrella, not that her residence near the fortress afforded free access to her father: for some time, she found it impossible to obtain even a momentary interview with the prisoner. But to breathe the same air with him,—and think of him nearer to herself, was some solace to her affliction. This was her first time of admittance into the long-interdicted citadel; and such is the origin of the delight which Charney sees beaming in her eyes, and the colour which he observes mantling on her cheek. Restored to the arms of her father, Teresa Girardi has indeed a right to look gay, and glad, and lovely!

It was a sentiment of curiosity which attracted her to the window;—a feeling of interest soon attaches her to the spot. The noble prisoner and his occupation excite her attention; but finding herself noticed in her turn, she tries to recede from observation, as if convicted of unbecoming boldness. Teresa has nothing to fear! The Count de Charney, engrossed by Picciola and her flower-bud, has not a thought to throw away on any rival beauty!

A week afterwards, when the young girl was admitted to pay a second visit to her father, she turned her steps, almost unconsciously, towards the grated window for a glimpse of the prisoner; when Girardi, laying his hand upon her arm, exclaimed, " My fellow-prisoner has not been near his plant these three days. The poor gentleman must be seriously ill."

" Ill; seriously ill!" exclaimed Teresa, with emotion.

" I have noticed more than one physician traversing the court: and from what I can learn from Ludovico, they agree only to a single point;—that the Count de Charney will die."

" Die!" again reiterated the young girl, with dilating eyes, and terror rather than pity expressed in her countenance. " Unhappy man — unhappy man!" Then turning towards her father, with terror in her looks, she exclaimed, " People DIE, then, in this miserable place !"

" Yes, the exhalations from the old moats have infected the citadel with fever."

" Father, dearest father !"

She paused — tears were gathering under her eyelids; and Girardi, deeply moved by her affliction, extended his hand tenderly towards her. Teresa seized and covered it with tears and kisses.

At that moment Ludovico made his appearance. He came to present to the fly-catcher a new captive whom he had just arrested: —neither more nor less than a dragon-fly with golden wings, which he offered with a triumphant smile to Girardi. The fly-catcher smiled, thanked his gaoler, and, unobserved by Ludovico, set the insect at liberty; for it was the twentieth individual of the same species, with which he had furnished him during the last few days. He profited, however, by the gaoler's visit to ask tidings of his fellow-prisoner.

"*Santissimo mio padrono!* do you fancy I neglect the poor fellow?" cried Ludovico, gruffly: "though still under my charge, he will soon be under that of St. Peter. I have just been watering his favourite tree."

" To what purpose—since he is never to behold its blossoms ?" interrupted the daughter of Girardi.

" *Perche, damigella—perche ?*" cried the gaoler, with his accustomed wink, and sawing the air with a rude hand, of which the fore-finger was authoritatively extended; " because, though the doctors have decided that the sick man has taken an eternal lease of the flat of his back, I, Ludovico, gaoler of Fenestrella, am of a different opinion. *Non lo credo—troudidio!*—I have notions of my own on the subject."

And turning on his heel he departed; assuming, as he left the room, his big voice of authority, to acquaint the poor girl, that only twenty-two minutes remained of the time allotted for her visit to her father. And at the appointed minute, to a second, he returned, and executed his duty of shutting her out.

The illness of Charney was indeed of a serious nature. One evening, after his customary visit to Picciola, an attack of faintness overpowered him on regaining his room; when, rather than summon assistance, he threw himself on the bed, with aching brows, and limbs agitated by a nervous shivering. He fancied sleep would suffice for his restoration.

But instead of sleep, came pain and fever; and on the morrow, when he tried to rise, an influence more potent than his will nailed him to his pallet. Closing his eyes, the Count resigned himself to his sufferings. In the face of danger, the calmness of the philosopher and the pride of the conspirator returned. He would have felt dishonoured by a cry or murmur, or an appeal to the aid of those by whom he was sequestered from the breathing world;—contenting himself with instructions to Ludovico respecting the care of his plant, in case he should be detained in bed, the *carcere duro* which was to render still harder his original captivity. Physicians were called in, and he refused to reply to their questioning. Charney seemed to fancy that, no longer master of his existence, he was exempted from all care for his life. His health was a portion of his confiscated property; and those who had appropriated all, might administer to *that* among the rest. At first, the doctors attempted to overcome his spirit of perversity; but finding the sick man obstinately silent, they began to interrogate his disorder instead of his temper.

The pathognomonic symptoms to which they addressed themselves, replied in various dialects and opposite senses; for the learned doctors invested their questions, each in the language of a different system. In the livid hue of Charney's lips, and the dilated pupils of his eyes, one saw symptoms of putrid fever; another, of inflammation of the viscera; while the third inferred, from the coloration of the neck and temples, the coldness of the extremities, and the rigidity of the countenance, that the disorder was paralytic or apoplectic;—protesting that the silence of the patient was involuntary, the result of the cerebral congestion.

Twice did the captain-commandant of the fortress deign to visit the bedside of the prisoner. The first time to inquire whether the Count had any personal requests to make,—whether he was desirous of a change of lodging, or fancied the locality had exercised an evil influence over his health; to all which questions Charney replied by a negative movement of the head. The second time, he came accompanied by a priest. The Count had been given over by his doctors as in a hopeless state. His time was expired; it became necessary to prepare him for eternity; and the functions of the commandant required that he should see the last consolations of religion administered to his dying prisoner.

Of all the duties of the sacerdotal office, the most august, perhaps, are those of the ordinary of a prison—of the priest whose presence sanctifies the aspect of the gibbet! Yet the scepticism of modern times has flung its bitter mockeries in the face of these devoted men! " Hardening their hearts under the cuirass of habit," says the voice of the scorner, " these officials become utterly insensible. They forget to weep with the condemned,—they forget to weep for them; and the routine of their professional exhortations has neither grace nor inspiration in its forms of prayer."

Alas! of what avail were the most varied efforts of eloquence, —since the exhortation is fated to reach but once the ear of the victim!—Alas! what need to inveigh against a calling which condemns the pure and virtuous to live surrounded by the profligate and hard-hearted, who reply to their words of peace and love, with insults, imprecations, and contempt? Like yourselves, these devoted men might have tasted the luxuries and enjoyments of life, —instead of braving the contact of the loathsome rags of misery, and the infected atmosphere of a dungeon. Endued with human sensibilities, and that horror of sights of blood and death inherent in all mankind, they compel themselves to behold, year after year, the gory knife of the guillotine descend on the neck of the malefactor; and such is the spectacle, such the enjoyment, which men of the world denounce as likely to wear down their hearts to insensibility!

In place of this "man of sorrows and acquainted with grief," devoted for a lapse of years to this dreadful function, in place of this humble Christian, who has made himself the comrade of the executioner, summon a new priest to the aid of every criminal! It is true, he will be more deeply moved; it is true, his tears will fall more readily;—but will he be more capable of the task of imparting consolation? His words are rendered incoherent by tears and sobs; his mind is distracted by agitation. The emotion of which he is so deeply susceptible, will communicate itself to the condemned; and enfeeble his courage at the moment of rendering up his life a sacrifice to the well-being of society. If the fortitude of the new almoner be such as enables him to command at once composure in his calling, be assured that his heart is a thousand times harder than that of the most experienced ordinary.

No,—cast not a stone at the prison priest; throw no additional obstacles in the way of so painful a duty!—Deprive not the condemned of their last friend. Let the cross of Christ interpose, as he ascends the scaffold, between the eyes of the criminal and the fatal axe of the executioner. Let his last looks fall upon an object proclaiming, trumpet-tongued, that after the brief vengeance of man, comes the everlasting mercy of God!

The priest summoned to the bedside of Charney, was fortunately worthy of his sacred functions. Fraught with tenderness for suffering humanity, he read at once, in the obstinate silence of the Count, and the withering sentences which disfigured his prison walls, how little was to be expected of so imperious and scornful a spirit; and satisfied himself with passing the night in prayers by his bedside, charitably officiating with Ludovico in the services indispensable to the sufferer. The Christian priest waited, as for the light of dawning day, an auspicious moment to brighten with a ray of hope the fearful darkness of incredulity!

In the course of that critical night, the blood of the patient determining to the brain, produced transports of delirium, necessitating restraint to prevent the unfortunate Count from dashing himself out of bed. As he struggled in the arms of Ludovico and the priest, a thousand incoherent exclamations and wild apostrophes burst from his lips; among which the words "*Picciola,—povera Picciola!*" were distinctly audible.

"*Andiamo!*" cried Ludovico, the moment he caught the sound. "The moment is come!—Yes, yes, the Count is right—the moment is come," he reiterated with impatience. But how was he to leave the poor chaplain there alone, exposed to all the violence of a madman? "In another hour, it may be too late!" cried Ludovico. "*Corpo di Dio!*—it will be too late. Blessed Virgin, methinks he is growing calmer! Yes, he droops!—he closes his eyes!—he is sinking to sleep! If at my return he is still alive, all's well. Hurra! reverend father, we shall yet preserve him, hurra, hurra!"

And away went Ludovico, satisfied, now the excitement of Charney's delirium was appeased, to leave him in the charge of the kind-hearted priest.

GILBERT & GIHON

In the chamber of death, lighted by the feeble flame of a flickering lamp, nothing now was audible but the irregular breathing of the dying man, the murmured prayers of the priest, and the breezes of the Alps whistling through the grating of the prison-window. Twice, indeed, a human voice mingled in these monotonous sounds:—the "*qui vive?*" of the sentinel, as Ludovico passed and repassed the postern on his way to his lodge, and back to the chamber of the Count. At the expiration of half an hour, the chaplain welcomed the return of the gaoler, bearing in his hand a cup of steaming liquid.

"*Santo Christo!*—I had half a mind to kill my dog!" said Ludovico, as he entered. "The brute, on seeing me, set up a howl, which is a sign of evil portent! But how have you been going on nere? Has he moved? No matter! I have brought something that will soon set him to rights!—I have made bold to taste it myself!—bitter, saving your reverence's presence, as five hundred thousand *diavoli!* Pardon me! *mio padre!*"

But the priest gently put aside the offered cup.

"After all," said Ludovico, "'tis not the stuff for us. A pint of good muscadello, warmed with a slice or two of lemon, is a better thing for sitters-up with the sick,—eh! *Signore Capellano?* But *this* is the job for the poor Count;—*this* will put things in their places. He must drink it to the last drop; for so says the prescription."

And, as he spoke, Ludovico kept pouring the draught from one cup to another, and blowing to cool it; till, having reduced it to the proper temperature, he forced the half-insensible Count to swallow the whole potion, while the chaplain supported his shoulders for the effort. Then, covering the patient closely up, they drew together the curtains of the bed.

"We shall soon see the effects," observed the jailer to his companion. "I don't stir from hence till all is right. My birds are safe locked in their cages; my wife has got the babe to keep her company. What say you, *Signore Capellano?*"

And Ludovico's garrulity having been silenced by the almoner, by a motion of the hand, the poor fellow stationed himself in silence at the foot of the bed, with his eyes fixed on the dying man; retaining his very breath in the anxiousness of his watchfulness for the event. At length, perceiving no sign of change in the Count, he grew uneasy. Apprehensive of having accelerated the last fatal change, he started up, and began pacing the room, snapping his fingers, and addressing menacing gestures to the cup, which was still standing on the table.

Suddenly he stopped short, and fixed his eyes on the livid face of Charney.

"I have been the death of him," cried he, accompanying the

apostrophe with a tremendous oath. "I have certainly been the death of him."

The chaplain raised his head, when Ludovico, unappalled by his air of consternation, began anew to pace the room, to stamp, to swear, to snap his fingers with all the energy of Italian gesticulation, till, tired out by his own impetuosity, he threw himself on his knees beside the priest, hiding his head in the bedclothes, and murmuring his *mea culpa*, till, in the midst of a paternoster, he fell asleep.

At dawn of day, the chaplain was still praying, and Ludovico still snoring; when a burning hand, placed upon the forehead of the latter, suddenly roused him from his slumbers.

"Give me some drink," murmured the faint voice of Charney.

And, at the sound of a voice which he had supposed to be for ever silenced, Ludovico opened his eyes wide with stupefaction to fix them on the Count, upon whose face and limbs the moisture of an auspicious effort of nature was perceptible. The fever was yielding to the effect of the powerful sudorific administered by Ludovico; and the senses of Charney being now restored, he proceeded to give rational directions to the gaoler, concerning the mode of treatment to be adopted; then, turning towards the priest, still humbly stationed on his knees at the bedside, he observed,—

"I am not yet dead, sir? Should I recover, (as I have every hope of doing,) present the compliments of the Count de Charney to his trio of doctors, and tell them I dispense with their further visits, and the blunders of a science as idle and deceptious as all the rest. I overheard enough of their consultations to know that I am indebted to chance alone for my recovery."

"*Chance!*" faltered the priest—"chance!"—And, having raised his eyes to Heaven in token of compassion, they fell upon the fatal inscription on the wall—

"CHANCE, THOUGH BLIND, IS THE SOLE AUTHOR OF THE CREATION."

The chaplain paused, after perusing this frightful sentiment; then, having gathered breath by a deep and painful inspiration, he added, in a solemn voice, the last word inscribed by Charney.—

"*Perhaps!*"

And ere the startled Count could address him, he had quitted the apartment.

CHAPTER VII.

ELATED by success, Ludovico lent his ear, in a sort of idiotic ecstasy, to every syllable uttered by the Count. Not that he comprehended their meaning:—*There*, luckily, he was safe. But his dead man was alive again; had resumed his power of speaking, thinking, acting,—a sufficient motive of exultation and emotion to the delighted gaoler.

"*Viva!*" cried he; "*viva, evviva.* He is saved. All's well! *Che maraviglia!* Saved!—and thanks to whom?—*to what?*"

And, waving in the air his earthen vessel, he proceeded to hug and embrace it, saluting it with the tenderest diminutives of the Tuscan vocabulary.

"Thanks to what?" echoed the sick man. "Why, to your friendly care, my good Ludovico. Nevertheless, should my cure be perfected, you will find those doctors yonder claiming all honour for their prescriptions; and the priest for his prayers."

"Neither they nor I have any title to the victory," cried Ludovico, with still wilder gesticulation. "As to the *Signore Capellano, his* handiwork may have done something: 'tis hard to say. But as to the other,— ay, ay, — as to the other bringer of salvation—"

"To whom do you allude?" interrupted Charney, expecting that the superstitious Ludovico would attribute his recovery to the interposition of some favourite saint. "*Who* has deigned to become my protector?"

"Say *protectress*, and you will be nearer the mark," cried Ludovico.

"The Madonna,—eh?" demanded Charney, with an ironical smile.

"Neither saint nor Madonna!" replied the gaoler, stoutly. "She who has preserved you from the jaws of death and the claws of Satan, (for dying without confession you were damned as well as dead,) is no other than my pretty little god-daughter."

"Your god-daughter!" said the Count, lending a more attentive ear to his rhapsodies.

"Ay, *Eccellenza*, my god-daughter, *Picciola, Picciolina, Picciolctta.* Was not I the first to baptize your favourite? Did I not give her the name of *Picciola?* Have you not often told me so yourself? Ergo, — the plant is my god-daughter, and I her god-father — *per Bacco!* I'm growing proud of the distinction!"

"*Picciola!*" exclaimed Charney, starting up, and resting his elbow on his pillow, while an expression of the deepest interest took possession of his countenance. "Explain yourself, my good Ludovico, explain yourself!"

"Come, come, no shamming stupid, my dear lord!" said the gaoler, resuming the customary wink of the eye, "as if 'twas the first time that she had saved your life!"

"The first time?"

"Didn't you tell me yourself that the herb was the only specific against the disorder to which you were subject? Lucky job I hadn't forgotten it; for the Signora Picciola proves to have more wisdom in one of her leaves, than the whole faculty of Montpellier in the noddles that fill its trencher-caps. *Trondidio,* my little god-daughter is able to defeat a regiment of doctors! ay, in full complements — four battalions, and four hundred picked men to each. Pray, did not your three humbugs in black, throw back the coverlid on your nose, and pronounce you to be a dead man? while Picciola, the stout-hearted little weed, (God send her seed in her harvest!) brought you round in the saying of a paternoster? 'Tis a recipe I mean to keep like the apple of my eye; and if ever poor little Antonio should fall sick, he shall drink broths of the herb, and eat salads of it; though, good truth, 'tis as bitter as wormwood. A single cup of the infusion, and all acted like a charm. *Vittoria! Viva l'illustrissima Signorina Picciola!*"

Charney had not the heart to resent these tumultuous ecstacies of his worthy keeper. The idea of being indebted for his life to the agency of the feeble favourite, which had embellished his days of health, insensibly brought a smile to his still feverish lips. But a vague apprehension oppressed his feelings.

"In what way, my good Ludovico, did you manage to apply your remedy?" said he, faintly.

"Faith! easily enough! A pint of scalding water poured upon the leaves," (Charney bit his lips with anxiety,) "in a close kettle, which, after a turn or two over the stove, furnished the decoction."

"Indeed!" exclaimed the Count, falling back on his pillow, and pressing his hand to his forehead. "You have then destroyed the plant! I must not reproach you, Ludovico; you did it for the best. And yet, my poor *Picciola!* What will become of me, now I have lost my little companion!"

"Come, come! compose yourself!" answered Ludovico, assuming the paternal tone of a father comforting his child for the loss of a favourite plaything. "Compose yourself, and do not expose your limbs to cold, by throwing off your clothes in this way. Listen to reason!" he continued, disposing the covering round the person of his patient. "Was I to hesitate between the life of a gillyflower and the life of a *man?* Certainly not! 'Twould have been a sin—a murder!"

Charney groaned heavily.

"However, I hadn't the heart to plunge the poor thing head foremost into the smoking kettle. I thought a loan might do as well as total pillage; so, with my wife's scissors, I snipped off leaves enough for a strong infusion, (sparing the buds; for the jade has now *three* flower-buds for her top-knot,) and though her foliage is a little the thinner, I've a notion the plant will not suffer from thinning. *Picciola* will, perhaps, be the better for the job, as well as her master. So now, be prudent, *eccellenza!* only be prudent, and all will go by clock-work at Fenestrella."

Charney, directing a glance of grateful affection towards his gaoler, extended towards him a hand which, *this* time, Ludovico felt himself privileged to accept; for the eyes of the Count were moistened by tears of emotion. But suddenly recollecting himself, and angry with his own infraction of the rule he had traced for his conduct towards those committed to his charge, the muscles of Ludovico's dark face contracted, and he resumed his harsh, surly, every-day tone. Though still holding within his own the hand of his prisoner, he affected to give a professional turn to his attitude.

"See!" cried he, "in spite of my injunctions, you still persist in uncovering yourself. Remember, sir, I am responsible for your recovery!"

And, after further remonstrances, made in the dry tone of office, Ludovico quitted the room, murmuring to the accompaniment of his rattling keys, the burden of his favourite song:

> "I'm a gaoler by my trade;
> A better ne'er was made.
> Easy 'tis to laugh for those that win, man
> I'd rather turn the key
> Than have it turn'd on me.
> Better out of doors than always in, man!
> With a lira-lira-la,—driva din, man!"

CHAPTER VIII.

DURING the remainder of that and the following day, Charney exhibited the depression of mind and body which results from every great physical crisis. But on the third day he resumed his powers of thought and action; and, if still detained by weakness on his pillow, the time was not far distant when he was likely to resume his former habits of life.

What delight to renew his acquaintance with his benefactress!

All his thoughts were now turned towards Picciola!—There seemed to be something beyond the common course of events in the fact that a seed, accidentally shed within the precincts of his prison, should have germinated in order to cure in the first instance his moral disorder,—ennui: and in the second, the perilous physical disease to which he had been about to fall a victim. He, whom the splendour of wealth had failed to enliven,—he whom the calculations of human learning had failed to restore,—had been preserved, first and last, by a plant!—Enfeebled by illness, he was no longer able to apply his full force of reasoning to the developement of the question; and a superstitious feeling, accordingly, began to attach him with redoubled force to the mysterious PICCIOLA. It was impossible to ground upon a rational basis his sentiments of gratitude towards a non-sentient being; nevertheless Charney found it impossible to refuse his affection in exchange for the existence bestowed upon him. Where reason is paralysed, imagination exercises her influence without restraint. Charney's regard for his benefactress now became exalted into a religious feeling, or rather into a blind superstition. Between him and his favourite there existed a mysterious sympathy of nature, like the attraction which draws together certain inanimate substances. He even fancied himself under a charm,—a spell of enchantment. Who knows? Perhaps the arrogant refuter of the existence of a GOD, is about to fall into the puerilities of judicial astrology. For in the secrecy of his cell, Charney does not hesitate to apostrophize Picciola as his star,—his destiny,—his talisman of light and life!

It is a curious fact that scarcely one illustrious man, remarkable for knowledge or genius, convicted of doubt in the agency of a Providence, but has been in his own person the slave of superstition: while attempting to throw off the yoke of servitude, submitting to become threefold slaves. In the blind eagerness of their pride to arrogate to their own merit the power or glory they have attained,—those deep-seated instincts of religion which they have attempted to stifle in their souls,—thrust out of their natural channel,—force a way of their own towards daylight, and acquire a wild and irregular character. The homage they arrest in its course to heaven, falls back upon the earth. They would fain judge, though they refuse to believe: and the genius whose horizon they have circumscribed, requites the forced contraction by seeing things in part instead of a whole, and losing all power of estimating the homogeneous design of the great Master of all! They attach themselves to details, because an isolated fact is within the scope of their judgment: and do not so much as notice the points of union which connect it with universal nature. For what is the whole creation,—earth, air, water,—the winds, the waves, the stars,—mankind,—the universe, but an infinite being, complete, premeditated, varied into inscrutable details, and breathing and palpitating under the omnipresent hand of God?

Subdued, however, by the strength of his pride and the weakness of his health, Charney saw nothing to admire in nature but his weed,—his plant,—his Picciola; and, as if to justify his folly by analogy, dived into the vast stores of his memory for a precedent.

He called to mind all the miraculous plants recorded from the earliest times, by poet or historian; the *holly* of Homer, — the palm-tree of Latona, — the oak of Odin; — nay, even the golden herb which shines before the eyes of the ignorant peasants of Brittany, and the May-flower, which preserves from evil thoughts the simple shepherdess of La Brie. He recollected the sacred fig-tree of the Romans,—the olive of the Athenians,—the Teutatés of the Celts,—the vervain of the Gauls,—the lotus of the Greeks, —the beans of the Pythagoreans,—the mandrake of the Hebrews. He remembered the green campac which blossoms everlastingly in the Persian's paradise;—the touba tree which overshadows the celestial throne of Mahomet; — the magic camalata, the sacred amreet on whose branches the Indians behold imaginary fruits of Ambrosia and of voluptuous enjoyment. He recurred with pleasure to the symbolical worship of the Japanese, who elevate the altars of their divinities on pedestals of heliotropes and water-lilies, assigning the throne of Love himself to the corolla of a nenuphar. He admired the religious scruples of the Siamese, which make it sacrilege to exterminate or even mutilate certain consecrated shrubs. A thousand superstitions which in former times excited his pity and contempt toward the short-sightedness of human nature, tended now to elevate his fellow-creatures in his estimation. For the Count had discovered that, from the vegetation of an humble flower, may emanate lessons of wisdom; and doubted not, that all these idolatrous customs must have originated in sentiments of gratitude unexampled by tradition.

"From his imperial throne of the west," thought Charney, "Charlemagne did not disdain to exhort the nation submitted to his rule, to the culture of flowers. And have not Ælian and Herodotus recorded that the great Xerxes himself took such delight in the beauty of an oriental plane-tree, as to caress its stem,—press it tenderly in his arms,—sleep enraptured under its shade,—decorating it with bracelets and chains of gold, when compelled to bid adieu to his verdant favourite?"

As the convalescence of the Count proceeded, he was seated one morning reclining absorbed in thought in his own chamber of which he had not yet ventured to cross the threshold, when his door was suddenly burst open, and Ludovico, with a radiant countenance, hastened towards him.

"Vittoria!" cried he. "The creature is in bloom. *Picciola!* —*Picciolitta!—figlioccia mia!*"

"In bloom?" cried Charney, starting up. "Let me see her.— I *must* see the blossom."

In vain did the worthy gaoler represent the imprudence of going too soon into the air; and implore the Count to delay the undertaking for a day or two. The morning was uncertain,—the atmosphere chilly. A relapse might bring the invalid once more to the gates of death. But Charney was deaf to all remonstrance! He consented only to wait an hour, in order that the sun might become one of the party.

"Picciola is in bloom!" repeated Charney to himself. And how long,—how tedious did that hour appear, which was still to divide him from the darling of his imagination! For the first time since his illness, he judged it necessary to dress. He chose to dedicate his first toilet to Picciola in bloom. He actually looked into his pocket-glass while he arranged his hair to do honour to his visit to a flower!—A *flower?*—Nay!—surely something more? His visit is that of the convalescent to his physician,— of the grateful man to his benefactress,—*almost* of the lover to his mistress! He was surprised to notice in the glass the ravages which care and sickness had wrought in his appearance. He began to suspect, for the first time, that bitter and venomous thoughts may tend to canker the human frame; and milder contemplations produce a more auspicious temperament.

At the appointed moment, Ludovico reappeared, to offer to the Count de Charney the support of his arm down the steep steps of the winding stone staircase; and scarcely had the sick man emerged into the court, when the emotion caused by a sudden restoration to light and air, operating on the sensitiveness of an easily excitable nervous system, produced a conviction on his mind that the whole atmosphere was vivified and embalmed by the emanations of his flower. It was to Picciola he attributed the delightful emotions which agitated his bosom.

The enchantress had, indeed, attired herself in all her charms! The coquette was shining in all her beauty. Her brilliant and delicately streaked corolla, in which crimson, pink, and white were blended by imperceptible gradations, her large transparent petal bordered by a little silvery fringe or ciliation, which the scattered rays of the sun seemed to brighten into a halo encircling the flower, exceeded the utmost anticipations of the Count, as he stood gazing with transport upon his queen! He feared, indeed, to tarnish the delicacy of the blossom by the contact of his hand or breath. Analysis or investigation seemed out of the question, engrossed as he was by love and admiration for the delicate thing whose fragrance and beauty breathed enchantment upon every sense!

But he was soon startled from his reveries! The Count noticed, for the first time, traces of the mutilation by which he had been restored to health; branches half cut away, and fading leaves still wounded by contact with the scissors of Ludovico. Tears started into his eyes! Instead of admiration for the delicate lines and perfumes of those expanding blossoms, he experienced only gratitude for the gift of life! He beheld a benefactress in his Picciola.

CHAPTER IX.

THE physician of the prison condescended to authorize on the morrow, the Count de Charney's resumption of his daily exercise. He was allowed the freedom of the little court, not only at the usual hours, but at any moment of the day. Air and exercise were considered indispensable to his recovery; and thus, the prisoner was enabled to apply himself anew to his long-interrupted studies.

In the view of committing to writing his scientific observations on the developement of his plant, from the moment of its germination, he tried to seduce Ludovico into furnishing him with pens and paper. He expected, indeed, to find the gaoler resume on this occasion an air of importance, and raise a thousand difficulties, but probably yield in the sequel out of love for his captive, or his god-daughter, or worldly pelf; for where perquisites were concerned, turnkey-nature was still uppermost. But to Charney's great surprise, Ludovico received his propositions with the most frank good-humour.

"Pens and ink? Nothing more easy, *Signor Conte!*" said he, tapping his pipe and turning aside his head to keep it alive by a whiff or two: for he made it a point to abstain from smoking in presence of the Count, to whom the smell of tobacco was disagreeable. "I, for my part, have no objection. But you see, such little tools as pens and paper remain under the lock and key of the governor, not under mine: and if you want writing materials, you have only to memorialize the captain-commandant, and your business is done!"

Charney smiled, and persevered.

"But in order to frame my petition, good Ludovico," said he, "pens, ink, and paper are, in the first instance, indispensable?"

"True, *eccellenza*, true! But we must drag back the donkey

by the tail to make it get on — no uncommon method with petitions," quoth the gaoler, half aside, crossing his hands consequentially behind him. "I must go straight to the governor, and tell him you have a request to make, no matter about what. That is not my business, but his and yours. If inconvenient to him to visit you in person, he 'll send his man of business, who will furnish you with a pen and a piece of stamped paper, just one sheet, ruled in form for a petition, on which you must inscribe your memorial in his presence; after which, he places his seal on it in yours; you return the pen to him, he makes you a bow, and away he goes with the petition!"

"But it is not from the governor I ask for paper, Ludovico, 'tis from yourself."

"From me? You don't then happen to know my orders?" replied the gaoler, resuming his accustomed severity. Then drawing a deep breath of his pipe, he exhaled the smoke with much deliberation, eyeing the Count askance during the process, turned on his heel, and quitted the room.

Next day, when Charney returned to the charge, Ludovico contented himself with winking his eye, shaking his head, and shrugging his shoulders. Not a word now was to be extracted from him.

Too proud to humiliate himself to the governor, but still bent upon his project, Charney now set to work to make a pen for himself out of a crow-quill tooth-pick. With some soot, carefully dissolved in one of the golden cups of his dressing-case, he furnished himself with ink and inkstand; while his cambric handkerchiefs, relics of a former splendour, were made to serve for writing-paper. With these awkward materials, he resolved to record the peculiarities of Picciola; occupying himself, even when absent from his favourite, with details of her life and history.

What profound remarks already presented themselves for inscription! What pleasure would Charney have found in communicating his observations to any intelligent human being! His neighbour, the fly-catcher, might have been a satisfactory auditor; for Charney had now found occasion to admire the bland and benevolent expression of a countenance, at first sight commonplace. Whenever the old man stood contemplating from his little window, with an inquiring and propitious eye, the beauty of Picciola, and the attentions of her votary, the Count felt irresistibly attracted towards his fellow-prisoner. Nay, smiles and salutations with the hand had been exchanged between them; and it was only the rigid interdiction of all intercourse between prisoners at Fenestrella, which prevented mutual inquiries after each other's health and pursuits. The solitary explorers into the mysteries of nature were therefore compelled to keep to themselves their grand discoveries in botany and entomology.

First among those by which Charney was interested, after the flowering of his plant, was the faculty exhibited by Picciola of turning her sweet face towards the sun, and following him with her looks throughout his daily course, as if to imbibe the greatest possible portion of his vivifying rays. When clouds obscured the orb of day, or there was a prospect of rain, her petals instantly closed, like a vessel furling its canvass before a storm. "Are light and heat so necessary, then, to her existence?" mused the Count; " and why should she fear to refresh herself with a sprinkling shower? Why? why? Picciola will explain! I have perfect confidence in Picciola!"

Already his darling had fulfilled towards him the functions of a physician. She was now about to become his compass and barometer, perhaps even his timepiece; for by dint of constantly inhaling her fragrance, Charney found he could discover that her perfumes varied in power and quality at different hours of the day. At first, this phenomenon seemed an illusion; but reiterated experiments convinced him that he was not mistaken; and he was soon able to designate to a certainty the hour of the day, according to the varying odour of the flower.*

Innumerable blossoms already studded his beautiful plant: towards evening, their exhalations were as delicious as they were potent; and at that moment, what a relief to the weary captive to draw near to his favourite! He now constructed a rude bench, with some planks derived from the munificence of Ludovico, and pointed a few logs, which he contrived to insert into the interstices of the pavement. A rough plank, nailed transversely, afforded him a leaning place, as he sat for hours musing and meditating in the fragrant atmosphere of his plant. He was happier there than he had ever felt on his silken ottomans of former days; and hour after hour would he sit reflecting on his wasted youth, which had elapsed without the attainment of a single real pleasure, or genuine affection! withering away in the midst of vain chimeras and premature satiety.

Often, after such retrospections, Charney found himself gradually soothed into reveries between sleep and waking; his senses subdued into a sort of apathetic torpor, his imagination excited to a visionary ecstacy, perplexing the desolate Count with scenes of days past and days to come.

He sometimes fancied himself in the midst of those brilliant fêtes, where, though himself the victim of ennui, he used to lavish

---

* Sir James Smith notices this property in the *Antirrhinum repens*. *Flora Britannica* vol. ii. p. 638.

upon others all the pleasures and luxuries of life. He seemed to stand gazing, some night of the Carnival, beside the illuminated façade of his hotel in the Rue de Verneuil; the rolling of a thousand carriages vibrating in his ear. One by one, they entered, by torchlight, his circular courtyard, depositing successively in the vestibule, covered with rich carpets, and protected by silken hangings, the fashionable belles of the day, enveloped in costly furs, under which was audible the rustling of satin or brocade; the beaux of the imperial court, with their high-crowned hats, cravats up to their ears, and redundant knee-strings; artists of eminence, with naked throats, Brutus-heads, and a costume half French, half Greek; and men of science or letters, wearing the distinctive academic collar of green. A crowd of lacqueys clustered on all sides, insolently defying, under their new liveries, the absolute decrees of the once puissant conventional republic of France.

The fancy of Charney next ascended to the crowded saloons in which were assembled all that was illustrious or notorious of the capital. The toga and chlamyda were jumbled together with jackets, or frock-coats. High-heeled shoes, with rosettes, trod the same floors as jockey-boots, with spur on heel, nay, even with the caliga and cothurnus. Men of the law, the pen, the sword, moneyed men and moneyless, artists and ministers of state, all were confounded in this *olla podrida* of the Directory. An actor stood hand in glove with an ex-bishop, a *ci-devant* peer with a *ci-devant* pauper; aristocracy and democracy were united like twin brothers; wealthy ignorance paraded itself arm in arm with starving erudition. Such was the regeneration of society, rallying round a common centre in masses, of which each felt itself still too feeble to stand alone. The marshalling of the crowd was deferred to some more convenient season; there would be a time for that hereafter! Such is the system of a play-ground, where all classes of a school mingle together under the impulse of a common thirst after amusement. As the boys grow older, the powerful influence of the spirit of social order insensibly estranges them from unbecoming companions, and high and low mechanically range themselves under their appointed banners.

With a silent smile did Charney contemplate this phantasmagoric display of piebald civilization. That which had once excited the bitter sneers of the man of the world, now served to divert him, as the memento of the wasted years spent by his native country in shallow, theoretic experiments, exposing it to the contempt of Europe.

At times, brilliant orchestras appeared to strike into animating and joyous measures; and lo! the opening of the ball!—Charney fancied he could recognise the favourite airs of former days, but more impressive than at their first hearing. The glittering radiance of the lustres, their prismatic reflection in the numerous mirrors, the soft and perfumed atmosphere of a ball-room—the aroma of a banquet—the mirth of the guests—the wild hilarity of the waltzers, who rustled against him in the mazy round,—the light and frivolous topics which excited their merriment, all tended to stimulate him to a degree of joyousness such as the reality of the dream had never succeeded in producing.

Women, too,—ivory-shouldered, slender-waisted, swan-throated,—women, arrayed in sumptuous brocades, gauzes striped with gold, and gems of sparkling lustre, thronged around him, smiling as they returned his salutations. One by one, he recognised those lovely beings; the grace and ornaments of his entertainments, when, opulent and free, the Count de Charney was cited as one of the favoured ones of the earth. There figured, unrivalled, the majestic Tallien, arrayed in the classic tunic of Greece, and covered with gems and costly rings, even to the toes of a foot from which might have been modelled that of some Venus of antiquity, naked but for the slight concealment of a golden sandal; the fair Recamier, to whom Athens would have erected altars; and Josephine, *ci-devant* Countess of Beauharnois, who, by dint of grace and affability, often passed for the fairest of these three graces of the Consulate. But even by the side of these, a hundred lovely women distinguished themselves, by their beauty or their elegance; and how exquisite did they now appear in the dreaming eyes of Charney! How much fairer, how much softer, than when they courted his smiles! How gladly had he *now* commanded liberty of choice among so many consummate enchantresses!

Sometimes, in the wildness of his reveries, he *did* venture on selection!—from the brilliant crowd he singled out one,—undistinguished, however, by the lustre of ivory shoulders, or a tiara of diamonds. Simple in attire as in deportment, *his* beauty lingered behind the rest, with downcast eyes, and cheeks suffused with blushes; a girl, a young girl, arrayed in simple white, and the no less spotless array of perfect innocence. She had never shone in his galas of other times; though now she stood out prominent on the canvass, while all others vanished into shade. At last, she seemed alone; and Charney began to reconsider her, charm by charm, feature by feature. His feelings were gently agitated by the lovely vision. But how much more when, on raising his eyes to the dark braids of her raven hair, he beheld a flower blooming there, *his* flower, the flower of Picciola! Involuntarily he extended his arms towards the beauteous apparition, when, lo! all grew confused and misty; and the distant music of the orchestra became once more audible, as the fair maiden and fair flower appeared to melt into each other. The fragrant corolla, expanding, enclosed with its delicate petals the loveliest of human faces, till all was hidden from his view. Instead of the gorgeous hangings and gilded walls of the ball-room, a hovering exhalation presented itself to the eyes of the Count. The lustres gradually extinguished, vanished in the distance, emitting a feeble arch of light on the outskirts of the gathering clouds. Rude pavement replaced the smooth and lustrous floor; stern Reason re-appeared to take possession of her throne; and the gracious illusions of fancy expired at her approach. A touch of the fatal wand of Truth dispelled at once the dream of the captive.

Charney woke to find himself musing on his rustic bench, his feet resting on the stones of the court-yard, and the daylight fading over his head. But Picciola,—thanks be to Heaven, Picciola is still before him!

The first time the Count became conscious of this species of vertigo, he noticed that it was only when meditating in the atmosphere of his plant that such gentle visions descended upon his mind. He recollected that the emanations of certain flowers are of so intoxicating a nature as even to produce asphyxia. It was, therefore, under the influence of his favourite, that these delicious dreams visited his imagination; and for his fête—his houries—his banquets—his music—he was still indebted to Picciola.

But the fair girl—the modest, gentle girl by whose image he had been so powerfully impressed—from whence has he derived *her* image? Did he ever behold her among the haunts of men? Is she, like the other divinities of his dream, the creature of reminiscence? Memory had nothing to reply! The past afforded no prototype for her charms! But the future;—if the vision his fancy has created should be the creature of anticipation, of presentiment rather than of recollection? alas! of what avail anticipations—of what avail revelations of the future to the unfortunate Charney! In a sentence of imprisonment for life, the destinies of the captive are accomplished.

All human hope, therefore, must be laid aside. The young girl of blooming blushes, and draperies of virgin white, shall be the Picciola of his imagination;—Picciola in the poetical personification of a dream;—his idol, his love, his bride. The sweet countenance and graceful form revealed to him, shall image forth the guardian spirit of his plant: with that, his reveries shall be brightened, and the aching void in his heart and soul filled up for ever! She shall dwell with him, muse with him, sit by his side, accompany his lonely walks, reply to him, smile upon him, enchant him with her ethereal love! She shall share his existence, his breath, his heart, his soul. He will converse with her in thought, and close his eyes to gaze upon her beauty! They shall form but one, in order that he may be alone no longer.

These emotions superseded the graver studies of the prisoner of Fenestrella, the enjoyments of the heart succeeding to those of the mind. Charney now gave himself up to all that poetry of existence, from whose sphere the soul returns laden with perfumes, as the bee, after extracting from the breast of the flower a harvest of honey. There was a life of daily hardship and captivity to be endured; there was a life of love and ecstacy to be enjoyed; and united, though apart, they completed the measure of existence of the once envied, but most unhappy Count de Charney. His time was shared between Picciola, his mortal flower—and Picciola, his immortal love: to reason, or rather reasoning, succeeded happiness and love!

CHAPTER X.

INDUCED at length to renew his experimental inquiries into the process of inflorescence, Charney became enchanted by the prodigious and immutable congruities of Nature. For some time, indeed, his eyes were baffled by the infinite minuteness of the phenomena to which his attention was directed; when, just as his patience became exhausted by his own incapacity, Ludovico conveyed to him, from his neighbour the fly-catcher, a microscopic lens, with which Girardi had been enabled to number eight thousand oculary facets on the cornea of a fly's eye.

Charney was transported with joy at the acquisition!—The most occult portion of the flower now became manifested for his investigation; and already he fancied himself advancing with gigantic strides in the path of science. Having carefully analyzed the texture of his flower, he convinced himself that the brilliant colours of the petal, their form, their crimson spots, the bands of velvet or satin which adorn their bases or fringe their extremities, are not intended for the mere gratification of the eye; but for the purpose of reflecting, attracting, or modifying the rays of the sun, according to the necessities of the flower during the grand process of fructification. The polished crowns or studs of the calyx, lustrous like porcelain, are doubtless glandular masses for the absorption of the air, light, and moisture, indispensable to the formation of the seed: for without light, no colour,—without air and moisture, no vitality. Moisture, light, and heat, are the elements of vegetable life, which, on its extinction, it bequeaths in restitution to the universe.

Unknown to Charney, his reveries and studies had attracted two deeply interested spectators; Girardi and his daughter. The latter, educated in habits of piety and seclusion, by a father imbued with reverential religious sentiments, was blessed with one of those ethereal natures, in which every good and holy interest seems united. The beauty and excellence of Teresa Girardi, the graces of her person and mind, had not failed to attract admirers; and her deep and expansive sensibility seemed to announce a predisposition for human affections. But if a vague preference had occasionally influenced her feelings amid the *fêtes* of Turin, every impulse of her gentle heart was now concentrated into grief for the captivity of her father.

Her soul was humbled,—her spirits subdued. Two only objects predominated in her heart: her father in prison,—her Saviour on the cross; despair on earth, but trust in immortality. Not that the fair daughter of Italy was of a melancholy mind. Her duties were easy to her, her sacrifices a delight; and where tears were to be dried or smiles awaked, there was the place of Teresa: hitherto, she had accomplished this task towards her father only; but from the moment of beholding Charney, his air of depression excited a two-fold compassion in her bosom. A captive like her father, and with her father, a mysterious analogy seemed to unite their destinies. But the Count is even more deserving pity than her father. The Count had no earthly solace remaining but a poor plant; and with what tenderness does he cultivate this last remaining affection! The noble countenance and fine person of the prisoner might, perhaps, unsuspected by Teresa, tend to enhance her compassion; but had she become acquainted with him in his days of splendour, when surrounded by the deceptious attributes of happiness, these would never have sufficed to distinguish him in her eyes. His isolation,—his abandonment,—his calamity,—his resignation, have alone attracted her interest, and prompted the gift of her tenderness and esteem. In her ignorance of men and things, Teresa is induced to include misfortune in her catalogue of virtues.

As bold in pursuance of a good action, as timid in personal deportment, she often directed towards Charney the good offices of her father; and one day when Girardi advanced to the window, instead of contenting himself, as usual, with a salutation of the hand, he motioned to the Count to draw as near as possible to the window; and, having moderated his voice to the lowest pitch, whispered—

"I have good news for you."

"And I my thanks to return," replied Charney, "for the microscope you have been kind enough to send me."

"It is rather to my daughter your thanks are due," replied Girardi. "It was Teresa who suggested the offer."

"You have a daughter; and are you allowed the happiness of seeing her?" demanded the Count, with interest.

"I am indeed so fortunate," replied the old man; "and return daily thanks to Heaven for having bestowed on me an angel in my child. During your illness, sir, none were more deeply interested in your welfare than my Teresa. Have you never noticed her at the grating, watching the care you devote to your flower!"

"I have some idea that——"

"But, in talking of my girl," interrupted the old man, "I neglect to acquaint you with important news. The Emperor is on his way to Milan, for his coronation as King of Italy."

"King of Italy!" reiterated Charney. "Doubtless, then, alas! to be our master. As to the microscope," continued the Count, who cares less for king or kaiser than for his ruling passion, "I have detained it too long: you may be in want of it. Yet, as my experiments are still incomplete, perhaps you will permit——"

"Keep it," interrupted the fly-catcher with a beneficent smile, perceiving, by the intonation of Charney's voice, with what regret he was about to resign the solace of his solitude, "keep it in remembrance of a companion in misfortune, who entertains a lively interest in your welfare."

Charney would have expressed his gratitude; but his generous friend refused all thanks. "Let me finish what I have to communicate, ere we are interrupted," said he. Then, lowering his voice again, he added, "It is rumoured that a certain number of prisoners will be released, and criminals pardoned, in honour of the coronation. Have you friends, sir, in Turin or Milan! Are there any to intercede for you?"

The Count replied by a mournful negative movement of the head. "I have not a friend in the world!" was his reply.

"Not a friend!" exclaimed the old man, with a look of profound pity. "Have you, then, exhibited mistrust of your fellow-creatures?—for friendship is unpropitious only to those who withhold their faith. I, Heaven be thanked, have friends in abundance,—good and faithful friends,—who might, perhaps, be more successful in *your* behalf than they have been in mine."

"I have nothing to ask of General Bonaparte," said Charney, in a harsh tone, characteristic of all his former animosities.

"Hush! speak lower! I hear footsteps," said Girardi.

There was an interval of silence; after which the Italian resumed, in a tone which softened, by almost paternal tenderness, the rebuke which it conveyed.

"Your feelings are still imbittered, my dear companion in adversity. Surely your study of the works of Nature ought to have subdued a hatred which is opposed to all the commandments of God, and all the chances of human happiness! Has not the fragrance of your flower poured balm into your wounds? The Bonaparte, of whom you speak so vindictively, surely I have more cause to hate him than yourself! My only son perished under his banner of usurpation."

"True! And did you not seek to avenge his death?"

"The false rumour, then, has reached you," said the old man, raising his head with dignity towards heaven, as if in appeal to the testimony of the Almighty. "*I* revenge myself by a deed of blood! No, sir! no! My utmost crime consisted in the despair which prompted me, when all Turin saluted the victor with acclamations, to oppose to them the cries of my parental anguish. I was arrested on the spot; a knife was found on my person, and I was branded with the name of assassin; *I*, an agonized father, who had just learned the loss of an only son."

"Infamous injustice! infamous tyranny!" cried the Count, with indignation.

"Nay," remonstrated Girardi, "I thank Heaven I am able to perceive that Bonaparte may have been deceived by appearances. His character is neither wicked nor cruel; or what was there to prevent him from putting us both to death? By restoring me to liberty, he would only atone an error; nevertheless, I should bless him as a benefactor. I find captivity, however, by no means insupportable. Full of trust in the mercy of Providence, I resign myself to the event; but the sight of my imprisonment afflicts my daughter; and for *her* sake I desire my liberation. I would fain shorten her exile from the world, her alienation from the pleasures of her age. Say! — have *you* no human being who sorrows over *your* misfortunes? — no *woman* who weeps for you in secret, to whom you would sacrifice even your *pride*, as an oppressed and injured man? Come, come, my dear brother in adversity! authorize my friends to include your name in their petitions!"

Charney answered with a smile, — "No woman weeps for me! no one sighs for my return: for I have no longer gold to purchase their affection. What is there to allure me anew into the world, where I was even less happy than at Fenestrella? But even were troops of friends awaiting me, — had I still wealth, honour, and happiness in store, — I would refuse the gift of freedom from that hand, whose power and usurpations I devoted myself to overthrow."

"You deny yourself even the enjoyment of hope?" said Girardi.

"Never will I bestow the title of emperor on one, who is either my equal or my inferior."

"Beware of sacrificing yourself to a sentiment, the offspring of vanity rather than of patriotism!" cried Girardi. "But peace! silence!" said he, more cautiously. "Some one approaches in earnest. *Addio*, away!" And the venerable Italian disappeared from the grated window.

"Thanks!—a thousand thanks for the microscope!" was Charney's last exclamation, as Girardi vanished from his view. And at that moment the door of the court-yard creaked on its hinges, and Ludovico made his appearance with the basket of provisions, forming the daily allowance of his prisoner. Observing the Count to be silent and absent, the gaoler accosted him only by rattling the plates, as he went by, as a signal that his dinner was ready. Then, having ascended to place all in order in the little chamber, amused himself, as he re-crossed the court, with making a silent obeisance to the *Signor* and *Signora*, as he was now in the habit of qualifying the Count de Charney, and his plant.

"The microscope is mine!" mused Charney, when he found himself alone. "But how have I merited such kind consideration on the part of a stranger? Ludovico, too, has become my friend. Under the rough exterior of the gaoler, beats a kind and noble heart. There exist, then, after all, virtuous and warm-hearted men. But where! *In a prison!*"

"Be thankful to adversity," remonstrated conscience, "which has made you capable of appreciating a benefit received. To what amounts the generosity of these two men? One of them watered your plant for you in secret; the other has conferred on you the means of analyzing its organization."

"In the smallest services consists the truest generosity," argued Charney, in reply.

"True," resumed the voice, "when such services are dedicated to your own convenience. Had Picciola never sprung to life, these two beings would have remained in your eyes,—the one a doting old man, engrossed by puerile pursuits; the other, a gross and sordid clod, absorbed by the love of gain. In your world of other days, Sir Count, to what, pray, did *you* attach yourself? To nothing. Your soul recoiled upon itself, and no man cared for you. By love comes love. It is your attachment to Picciola which has obtained you the affection of your companions. Picciola is the talisman by which you have attracted their regard."

Charney interrupted this mono-dialogue by a glance from the microscope towards Picciola. He has already forgotten the announcement of "Napoleon, Emperor of the French, and King of Italy!"—one half of which formerly sufficed to convert him into a conspirator and a captive. How unimportant in his eyes, now, those honours conferred by nations, and based upon the liberties of Europe! An insect hovering over his plant, threatening mischief to its delicate vegetation, seems more alarming than the impending destruction of the balance of power, by the conquests of a new Alexander.

CHAPTER XI.

ARMED with his glass, Charney now extended his field of botanical discovery; and, at every step, his enthusiasm increased. It must be owned, however, that inexperienced as he was in the method of scientific inquiry, devoid of first principles and appropriate instruments, he often found himself defeated; and the spirit of paradox became insensibly roused to existence by the cavilling temper of his mind.

He invented half a hundred theories on the circulation of the sap; on the coloration of the various parts of the flower; on the secretion of different kinds of aroma by different organs of the stem, the leaves, the flowers; on the nature of the gum and resin emitted by vegetables, and the wax and honey extracted by bees from the nectary. At first, ready answers suggested themselves to all his inquiries; but new systems arose, to confute on the morrow those of the preceding day. Nay, Charney seemed to take delight in the impotence of his own judgment, as if affording wider scope to the efforts of his imagination, and an indefinite term to the duration of his experiments and inferences.

A day of joy and triumph for the enthusiast was now approaching! He had formerly heard, and heard with a smile of incredulity, allusion to the loves of plants, and the sublime discoveries of Linnæus concerning vegetable generation. It was now his pleasing task to watch the gradual accomplishment of maternity in Picciola; and when, with his glass fixed on the stamens and pistils of the flower, he beheld them suddenly endowed with sensibility and action, the mind of the sceptic became paralyzed with wonder and admiration! By analogical comparison, his perceptions rose till they embraced the vast scale of the vegetable and animal creation. He recognised with a glance the mightiness, the immensity, the harmony of the whole. The mysteries of the universe seemed suddenly developed before him. His eyes grew dim with emotion,—the microscope escaped his hand. The atheist sinks back overpowered on his rustic bench, and after nearly an hour of profound meditation, the following apostrophe burst from the lips of Charney:—

"*Picciola!*" said he, in a tone of deep emotion,—"I had once the whole earth for my wanderings,—I was surrounded by those who called themselves my friends—by men of letters and science · and not one of the learned ever bestowed upon me as much instruc tion as I have received from thee!—not one of the friendly ever rendered me such good offices as thine! In this miserable courtyard, between the stones of whose rugged pavement thou hast sprung to life, I have reflected more, and experienced more profound emotions, than while traversing in freedom all the countries of Europe! Blind mortal that I have been!—When first I beheld thee, pale, feeble, puny, I looked on thee with contempt! And it was a companion that was vouchsafed to me—a book that was opened for my instruction—a world that was revealing itself to my wondering eyes! The COMPANION solaces my daily cares—attaching me to the existence restored me by her aid, and reconciling me with mankind, whom I had unfairly condemned. The BOOK teaches me to despise all works of human invention, convicting my ignorance, and rebuking my pride;—instructing me that science, like virtue, is to be acquired through lowliness of mind. Inscribed in the living characters of a tongue so long unknown to me, it contains a thousand enigmas, of which every solution is a word of hope. The WORLD is the region of the soul—the abstract and criterion of celestial and eternal nature :—the revelation of the organic law of love, from which results the order of the universe, the gravitation of atoms, the attraction of suns, and the electric union of all created things, from the highest star to the hyssop on the wall—from the crawling insect to man, who walks the earth with his brows elevated towards heaven—perhaps in search of the omnipotent Author of his being!"

The breast of Charney swelled with irrepressible emotion as he spoke. Thought succeeded thought in his brain; feeling after feeling arose in his heart;—till, starting from his seat, he began to traverse the court with hurried footsteps. At length, his agitation exhausted, he returned towards his Picciola, gazed upon her with ineffable tenderness, raised his eyes to heaven, and faintly articulated,—" Oh! mighty and unseen GOD!—the clouds of learning have too much confused my understanding,—the sophistries of human reason too much hardened my heart, for thy divine truths to penetrate at once into my understanding. In my unworthiness to comprehend thy glorious revelations, I can yet only call upon thy name, and humbly seek thy infinite, but invisible protection."

And with grave demeanour, Charney retraced his steps to his chamber; where the first sentence that met his eyes, inscribed with his own hand upon the wall, was—

"GOD is but a word!"

In another moment he had superadded to the inscription,—"a word, which serves perhaps to solve the great enigma of creation!"

"*Perhaps* —the master word of doubts, still disfigured the

phrase! — But it was something for the arrogant Charney to have arrived at *doubt*, from the extreme of absolute *negation*. He was recoiling in the path of falsehood he had so long pursued. He no longer pretended to rely for support upon his own strength, — his own faculties. He is willing now to learn, eager to perpetuate the soft emotions by which his pride has been subdued, and it is still to the insignificant Picciola he turns for instruction,—for a creed, —a GOD,—an immortality.

CHAPTER XII.

Thus passed the days of the prisoner; and after whole hours devoted to inquiry and analysis, Charney loved to turn from the weariness of his studies to the brightness of his illusions, — from Picciola the blooming plant, to Picciola the blooming girl. Whenever the awakening perfumes of his flower ascended to his chamber, oppressing his senses, and creating misty confusion before his eyes, he used to exclaim, " To-night Picciola will hold her court; I must hasten to Picciola."

Thus predisposed to reverie, his mind was promptly attuned into the sort of doze, in which, during the absence of reason, " mimic fancy wakes." Oh! were it not, indeed, a dearer enjoyment than any yet vouchsafed to human nature, if man could so far acquire authority over his dreams, as to live at will that secondary life where events succeed each other with such rapidity; where centuries cost us but one breathing hour; where a magic halo environs all the actors of the drama, and where nothing is real but the emotions of our thrilling hearts? Would you have music? Harmonious concerts might arise in spontaneous unison, unprefaced by discordant tuning, the anxious looks of the musicians, or the ungraceful and quaint forms of their instruments. Such is the world of dreams! Pleasure without repentance; the rainbow without the storm!

To such illusions did Charney resign himself! Faithful to the gentle image of his Picciola, it was to *her* he invariably appealed; and the vision came at his call, simple, modest, and beautiful, as at its first advent. Sometimes he surrounded her with the companions of his early studies; sometimes, united with his mother and sister, his imaginary love served to create around him the domestic happiness of his youth. Sometimes she seemed to introduce him into a dwelling cheered by competence, and adorned with elegance, where pleasures hitherto unknown, came wooing his enjoyment. After evoking the joys of memory and calling up reminiscences of the past, she gave existence to hope, to ties undreamed of, and joys unknown. Mysterious influence! Where was he to find the solution of the mystery? With the view of future comparison, the Count actually began to record on his cambric pages the wild illusions of his dreams!

One evening, in the midst of a flight of fancy, Picciola for the first time dispelled the charm of happiness and serenity, by the exercise of a sinister influence! At a later moment he recurred to the event as the effect of a fatal presentiment!

It was just as the fragrance of the plant indicated the sixth hour of evening, and Charney was musing at his accustomed post. Never had that aromatic vapour exercised its powers more potently: for more than thirty full-blown flowers were emitting the magnetic atmosphere, so influential over the senses of the Count. He fancied himself surrounded once more by the crowds of society; having drawn aside from which, towards an esplanade of verdure, his beloved Picciola deigned to follow his footsteps. The graceful phantom advanced smiling towards him; and Charney, in a musing attitude, stood admiring the supple grace of the young girl, around whose well-turned form the drapery of her snow-white dress played in harmonious folds, and her raven tresses, amid which bloomed the never absent flower! On a sudden he saw her start, stagger, and extend her arms towards him. He tried to rush towards her; but an insurmountable obstacle seemed to separate him from her side. A cry of horror instantly escaped his lips, and lo! the vision disappears! He wakes, but it is to hear a second cry, respondent to his own; yes, the cry, the voice of a female!

Nevertheless, the Count is still in his usual place — in the old court, and reclining on the rustic bench beside his Picciola! But at the grating of the little window, appeared the momentary glimpse of a female form! A soft and melancholy countenance, half hid in shade, seems gazing upon him; but when, rising from his seat, he hastens towards it, the vision vanishes, or rather the young girl hastens from the window. However swift her disappearance, Charney was able to distinguish her features, her hair, her form, the whiteness of her robe. He paused. Is he asleep or waking? Can it be that the insurmountable obstacle which divides him from Picciola is no other than the grating of a prison?

At that moment, Ludovico hastens towards him with an air of consternation.

"Are you again indisposed, *Signor Conte?*" cried the gaoler. " Have you had another attack of your old disorder? *Trondidio!* If we are obliged, for form's sake, to send for the prison doctor, I'll take care, *this* time, that no one but Madame Picciola and myself have a hand in the cure!"

" I am perfectly well," replied Charney, trying to recover his composure. " What put it into your head that I was indisposed?"

"The fly-catcher's daughter came in search of me. She saw you stagger, and hearing you cry aloud, fancied you were in need of assistance."

The Count relapsed into a fit of musing. It seemed to occur to him, for the first time, that a young girl occasionally inhabited that part of the prison.

" The resemblance I fancied I could discover between the stranger and Picciola, is doubtless a new delusion!" said he to himself. And he now recalled to mind Teresa's interest in his favour, mentioned to him by the venerable Girardi. The young Piedmontese had compassionated his condition during his illness. To *her* he is indebted for the possession of his microscope. His heart becomes suddenly touched with gratitude, and in the first effusion, a sudden remark seems to sever the double image, the young girl of his dreams, from the young girl of his waking hours; " Girardi's daughter wore no flower in her hair."

That moment, but not without hesitation, not without self-reproach, he plucked with a trembling hand from his plant a small branch covered with blossoms.

" Formerly," thought Charney, " what sums of money did I lavish to adorn, with gold and gems, brows devoted to perjury and shame! upon how many abandoned women and heartless men did I throw away my fortune, without caring more for them than for the feelings of my own bosom, which, at the same moment, I placed in the dust under their feet. Oh! if a gift derives its value from the regard in which it is held by the donor, never was a richer token offered by man to woman, my Picciola, than these flowers which I borrow from thy precious branches to bestow on the daughter of Girardi!"

Then, placing the blossomed bough in the hands of the gaoler, "Present these in my name to the daughter of my venerable neighbour, good Ludovico!" said he. "Thank her for the generous interest she vouchsafes me; and tell her that the Count de Charney, poor, and a prisoner, has nothing to offer her more worthy her acceptance."

Ludovico received the token with an air of stupefaction. He had begun to enter so completely into the passion of the captive for his plant, that he could not conjecture by what services the daughter of the fly-catcher had merited so distinguished a mark of munificence.

"No matter! *Capo di San Pasquali!*" exclaimed Ludovico, as he passed the postern. "They have long admired my god-daughter at a distance. Let us see what they will say to the brightness of her complexion, and sweetness of her breath, on a nearer acquaintance, *Picciolitta mia, andiamo!*"

CHAPTER XIII.

MANY sacrifices of a similar kind, however, were now required of Charney. The epoch of fructification is arrived. The brilliant petals of many of the flowers have fallen, and their stamens become useless: decaying, like the cotyledons, after the first leaves had attained maturity. The ovary containing the germ of the seeds begins to enlarge within the calyx. The fertile flowers lay aside their beauty, like matrons who, in achieving their maternal triumphs, begin to disdain for themselves the vain adornments of coquetry.

The Count now devotes his attention to the most sublime of all the mysteries of nature, the perpetuation of created kinds, and the reproduction of life. In opening and analyzing a bud detached some time before from the tree, by the injury of an insect, Charney had noticed the primary germ destined to fertilization, but demanding protection and nutriment from the flower before its feeble organization could be perfected. Admirable foresight of nature, as yet unexplained by the logic of science. But now the reproduction of a future Picciola is to be completed; and the narrow seed must be made to comprehend all the developement of a perfect plant. The curious observer is to direct his notice to the fecundation of the vegetable egg; and for this purpose, Picciola must be submitted to further mutilation. No matter!—She is already preparing herself for the reparation of her losses. On all sides, buds are reappearing. From every joint of her stem, or branches, new shoots are putting forth to produce a second flowering.

In pursuance of this task, Charney soon took his usual seat with the grave demeanour of an experimentalist. But scarcely had he cast his eyes upon the plant when he is shocked by the air of languor apparent in his favourite. The flowers inclining on their peduncles, seem to have lost their power of turning towards the sun; their leaves curling inwards their deep and lustrous verdure. For a moment Charney fancies that a heavy storm is at hand; and prepares his mats and osier bands to secure Picciola from the force of the wind or hail. But no! the sky is cloudless;—the air serene;—and the lark is heard singing out of sight, overhead, secure in the breathlessness of the blue expanse of heaven.

Charney's brow becomes overcast. "She is in want of water," is his first idea; but having eagerly fetched the pitcher from his chamber, and on his knees beside the plant, removed the lower branches, in order at once to reach the root, he is struck motionless with consternation. All—all—is explained. His Picciola is about to perish!

While the flowers and perfumes were multiplying to increase his studies and enjoyments, the stem of the plant, also, was increasing unobserved. Enclosed between two stones of the pavement, and strangled by their pressure, a deep indentation first gave token of her sufferings, the surface of which being at length crushed and wounded by the edges of the granite, the sap has begun to exude from the fissures, and the strength of the plant is exhausted!

Limited in the allotment of soil for her nutriment, her sap unnaturally expanded, her strength overtasked, Picciola must die, unless prompt relief can be afforded!—Her doom is sealed!—One only resource remains. By removing the stones that weigh upon her roots, the plant may yet be preserved. But how t. effect this, without an implement to assist her efforts?—Rushing towards the postern and knocking vehemently, the Count summons Ludovico to his aid. But although on the gaoler's arrival the explanation of the disaster and the sight of his expiring god-daughter overwhelm him with sorrow, no other answer can be obtained by Charney to his entreaties that the pavement may instantly be removed, than "*Eccellenza!* the thing is impossible!"

Without hesitation, the Count attempted to conciliate the gaoler's acquiescence by the offer no longer of the gilt goblet of his dressing-case, but the whole casket.

But Ludovico, assuming his most imposing attitude, folded his arms upon his breast; exclaiming, in his half-provincial, half-Piedmontese dialect, "*Bagasse, bagasse!* Ludovico is too old a soldier to submit to bribery. I know my orders. I know my duty. It is to the captain-commandant you must address yourself."

"No," cried Charney. "Rather would I tear up the stones with my hands, even were my bleeding nails sacrificed in the attempt!"

"Ay, ay! time will show!" replied Ludovico, resuming the pipe, which he was in the habit of holding half-extinguished under his thumb, during his colloquies with the Count; and after a puff or two, turning on his heel to depart.

"Good Ludovico!—I have hitherto found you so kind,—so charitable! Can you do nothing for my assistance?" persisted Charney.

"*Trondidio!*" answered the gaoler, trying to conceal by an oath the emotion gaining upon his feelings, "can't you leave me a moment's peace,—you and your cursed gilly-flower!—As to the *poverina*, I forgive her,—'tis no fault of Picciola!—but as to you, whose obstinacy will certainly be the death of the poor thing——"

"What would you have me do, then?" exclaimed the Count.

"Petition the commandant, I tell you, petition the commandant!" cried Ludovico.

"Never!"

"There you are again; but if your pride is so tetchy, will you give *me* leave to speak to him?"

"No," replied Charney; "I forbid you."

"*You* forbid me!" cried the gaoler:—"*D——e!* is it *your* orders I am to obey? If I choose to speak to him, who is to prevent me?"

"Ludovico!"

"Set your mind at ease; I am not going to undertake any such fool's errand. What business is it of mine?—Let her live, let her die;—*che m' importa?* If you want to put an end to the plant, 'tis your own affair—*Buona notte!*"

"But has your commandant sense enough to understand me?" demanded the Count, detaining him.

"Why not?—do you take him for a kinserlick? Tell him your story straight on end : pack it into pretty little sentences, like a

scholar who knows what he is about;—for now's the time to put
your learning to some use. Why shouldn't *he* enter into your love
for a flower as well as I have? Besides, I shall be there to put in
a word. I can tell him what a capital tisane is to be made of the
herb. The commandant's an ailing man himself. He has got a
sharp fit of the rheumatism upon him at this very moment, which
will perhaps make him enter into the case."

Charney still hesitated; but Ludovico pointed with one of his
knowing winks to Picciola, sick and suffering; and, with a gesture
of anxiety from the Count, off went the gaoler on his errand.

Some minutes afterwards, a man in a half-military, half-civil
uniform, made his appearance in the court, with an inkstand and a
sheet of paper bearing a government stamp. As Ludovico had
announced, this person remained present while Charney wrote out
his petition; received it sealed into his hands, and, with a respectful bow, departed, carrying off the inkstand.

Reader, despise not the self-abasement of the haughty Count de Charney!—marvel not at the readiness with which he has consented to an act of humiliation. Remember that Picciola is all in all to the poor prisoner! Reflect upon the influence of isolation on the firmest mind, the proudest spirit! Had he recourse to submission when *himself* oppressed with suffering, pining after the free air of liberty, overpowered by the walls of his dungeon, as Picciola by its pavement? No! for his own woes the Count had fortitude; but between himself and his favourite, a league of mutual obligation subsists—sacred enjoyments have arisen. Picciola preserved *his* life; must her own be sacrificed to his self-love?

The venerable Girardi presently beheld the Count pacing the little court with agitated footsteps, and gestures of anxiety and impatience. How tediously were the moments passing—how cruel the delay to which he was exposed! Three hours had elapsed since he despatched his petition; and no answer. As the sap of the expiring plant oozed from the wounded bark, Charney felt that he had rather his own blood were required of him. The old man, addressing him from the window, tried in vain to afford him consolation; but at length, more experienced than himself in accidents of the vegetable and animal kingdom, indicated a mode of closing up the wounds of the stem, so as to remove at least one source of peril.

With a mixture of finely chopped straw and moistened clay, he forms a mastic, easily fixed upon the bark with bandages of torn cambric. An hour passed rapidly in the performance; but at its close, the Count has to bewail anew the silence of the governor.

At the usual dinner hour, Ludovico made his appearance with a vexed and careworn countenance, annunciatory of no good tidings. The gaoler scarcely deigns a reply to the interrogations of Charney, except by monosyllables, or the roughest remonstrances.

"Can't you wait?—What use in so much hurry?—Give him time to write!"

Ludovico seemed preparing himself for the part which he found he should be required to play in the sequel.

Charney touched not a morsel: the sentence of life or death was impending over Picciola; and he sat trying to inspire himself with courage, by protesting that none but the most cruel of men could refuse so trifling a concession as he had asked. But his impatience did but increase with his arguments, as if the commandant could have no business more important in hand than to address an immediate answer to his memorial. At the slightest noise, Charney's eyes turned eagerly towards the door by which he was expecting the fiat of the governor.

Evening came—no news;—night—not a word! The unfortunate prisoner did not close his eyes that night!

CHAPTER XIV.

On the morrow, the anxiously expected missive was delivered to him. In the dry and laconic style of office, the commandant announced that no change could be made in the distribution of the walls, moats, or ditches of the fortress of Fenestrella, unless by the express sanction of the Governor of Turin; "and the pavement of the court," added the commandant, "is virtually a wall of the prison."

Charney stood confounded by the stupidity of such an argument!—To make the preservation of a flower a state question,— a demolition of the imperial fortification,— to wait a reply from the Governor of Turin!—wait a century, when a day's delay was likely to prove fatal! The governor might perhaps refer him to the prime minister,—the minister to the senate,—the senate to the emperor himself. What profound contempt for the littleness of mankind arose in his bosom at the idea!— Even Ludovico appeared little better in his eyes than the assistant of the executioner: for on the first outburst of his indignation, the gaoler remonstrated in the tone of an underling of the administration, replying to all his entreaties by citing the rules and regulations of the fortress.

Charney drew near to the feeble invalid whose bloom was already withering; and with what grief did he now contemplate her fading hues! The happiness — the poetry of his life seemed vanishing before him. The fragrance of Picciola already indicated a mistaken hour, like a watch whose movements are out of order. Every blossom drooping on its stem had renounced the power of turning towards the sun; as a dying girl closes her eyes that she may not behold the lover, the sight of whom might attach her anew to a world from which she is departing.

While Charney was giving way to these painful reflections, the voice of his venerable companion in captivity appealed to his attention.

"My dear comrade," whispered the mild and paternal accents of the old man, "if she should die, — and I fear her hours are numbered,—what will become of you here alone? What occupation will you find to fill the place of those pursuits that have become so dear to you? You will expire, in your turn, of lassitude and ennui; solitude once invaded, becomes insupportable in the renewal! You will sink under its weight, as I should, were I now parted from my daughter,—from the guardian angel whose smile is the sunshine of my prison. With respect to your plant, the Alpine breezes doubtless wafted hither the seed, or a bird of the air dropped it from his beak; and even were the same circumstance to furnish you with a second Picciola, your joy in the present would be gone, prepared as you would be to see it perish like the first. My dear neighbour, be persuaded!—suffer me to have your liberty interceded for by my friends. Your release will perhaps be more easily obtained than you are aware of. A thousand traits of clemency and generosity of the new emperor, are every where rumoured. He is now at Turin, accompanied by Josephine."

And this last name was pronounced by the old man as if it contained the promise of success.

"At Turin!"—exclaimed Charney, eagerly raising his drooping head.

"For the last two days," replied Girardi, delighted to see his advice less vehemently rejected than usual by the Count.

"And how far is it from Turin to Fenestrella?" continued Charney.

"By the Giaveno and Avigliano road, not more than seven leagues."

"What space of time is necessary for the journey?"

"Four or five hours, at the least: for at this moment the roads are obstructed by troops, baggage-wagons, and the equipages of those who are hastening to the approaching festival. The road that winds through the valleys by the river side, is certainly the longest; but in the end, would probably cause less delay."

"And do you think it possible," resumed Charney, "to procure a messenger for me who would reach Turin this very night?"

"My daughter would try to find a trustworthy person."

"And you say that General Bonaparte,—that the First Consul—"

"I said *the Emperor*,"—gravely interrupted Girardi.

"The Emperor, then,—you say that the Emperor is at Turin?" resumed Charney, as if gathering courage for some strong measure. "I will address a memorial, then, to the Emperor." And the Count dwelt upon the latter word, as if to accustom himself to the new road he had determined to follow.

"Heaven's mercy be praised!" ejaculated the old man: "for Heaven itself has inspired this victory over the instigations of sinful human pride!—Yes—write! let your petition for pardon be worded in proper form; and my friends Fossombroni, Cotenna, and Delarue, will support it with all their interest, with Marescalchi, the minister, with Cardinal Caprara, and even with Melzi, who has just been appointed chancellor of the new kingdom. Who knows? We may perhaps quit Fenestrella on the same day!—you to recommence a life of usefulness and activity,—I, to follow the gentle guidance of my daughter."

"Nay, sir—nay," cried the Count. "Forgive me if I decline the protection to which your good-will would generously recommend me. It is to the Emperor in person that my memorial must be remitted—to-night, or early in the morning. Do you answer to me for a messenger?"

"I do," said the old man, firmly, after a momentary pause.

"One question more," added Charney. "Is there no chance of your being compromised by the service you are so kind as to render me?"

"The pleasure of being of use to you leaves me no leisure for apprehension," answered Girardi. "Let me but lend my aid to the alleviation of your afflictions, and I am content. Should evil arise, I know how to submit to the decrees of Providence."

Charney was deeply touched by these simple expressions. Tears glistened in his eyes as he raised them towards the good old man.

"What would I give to press your hand!" cried he; and he stretched out his arm with the utmost effort, in hopes to reach the grated window, while Girardi extended *his* between the bars. But it was all in vain. A movement of mutual sympathy was the utmost that could pass between them.

When Charney took leave of Picciola, on his way to his chamber, he could not refrain from whispering, "Courage! I shall save thee yet!" And, having reached his miserable *camera*, he selected the whitest of his remaining handkerchiefs, mended his toothpick with the greatest care, made up a fresh supply of ink, and set to work. When his memorial was completed, which was not without a thousand pangs of wounded pride, a little cord descended from the grating of Girardi's window, to which the paper was attached by the Count, and carefully drawn up.

An hour afterwards, the person who had undertaken to present the petition to the Emperor, was proceeding, accompanied by a guide, through the valleys of Suza, Bussolino, and St. George, along the bank of the river Doria. Both were on horseback; but the greater their haste, the more perplexing the obstacles by which their way was impeded. Recent rains had broken away the bank; the river was, in many spots, overflowing; and more than one raging torrent appeared to unite the Doria with the lake Avigliano Already, the forges of Giaveno were reddening in the horizon, announcing that the day was about to close, when, joyfully regaining the high road, they entered, though not without having surmounted many difficulties, the magnificent avenue of Rivoli; and late in the evening, arrived at Turin. The first tidings by which they were saluted, was an announcement that the emperor-king had already proceeded to Alexandria.

7

BOOK II.

CHAPTER I.

At dawn of day, next morning, the city of Alexandria was arrayed in all its attributes of festivity. An immense population circulated in the streets, festooned with tapestry, garlands of flowers, and glossy foliage. The crowd pressed chiefly from the Town Hall, inhabited by Napoleon and Josephine, towards the triumphal arch, erected at the extremity of the suburb through which they were to pass on their way to the memorable plains of Marengo.

The whole way, from Alexandria to the Marengo, the same populace, the same cries, the same braying of trumpets. Never had the pilgrimage to the shrine of our Lady of Loretto—never had even the Holy Jubilee of Rome, attracted such multitudes as were proceeding towards the field of that tremendous battle, whose ashes were scarcely yet cold in the earth. On the plain of Marengo, the Emperor has promised to preside over a sham-fight—a mimic representation, given in honour of the signal victory obtained five years before upon the spot, by the Consul Bonaparte.

Tables, raised on trestles, appear to line the road. The people, in innumerable masses, are eating, drinking, singing, shouting, and acting plays in the open air. Even preaching is not neglected; for more than one pulpit has been improvisated between the theatres and wine-shops; from which hosts of greasy monks, not satisfied with giving their benediction to the passengers, and exhorting them to temperance and sobriety, gratify their avarice by the sale of consecrated chaplets, and little virgins, carved in ivory.

In the long and only street of the village of Marengo, every house, transformed into an inn, presents a scene of noise and confusion. To every window, the eyes of the spectators are attracted by strings of smoked hams or sausages; of quails or red partridges, or pyramids of gingerbread and cakes. People are pushing in, or pushing out at every door; Italians and French, soldiers or peasants; heaps of maccaroni, of marchpane, and other dainties, are beginning to disappear. In the dark and narrow staircases, people rub quarrelsomely against each other; some even compelled, by the rapacity of their neighbours, to raise over their heads the food they are carrying; while a cleverer hand and longer arm than their own, makes off, unperceived, with the savoury burden:—whether a buttered loaf, figs, grapes, oranges, a Turin ham, a larded quail, a force-meat pie, or an excellent *stufato*, in its tureen;—when cries of indignation, or shrieks of distress, accompanied by mockeries and loud laughter, resound on every side. The thief, in the ascending line upon the staircase, satisfied with his plunder, tries to turn back, and run away. The victim, in the descending line, robbed of his dinner, attempts to return, and furnish himself with new provisions; and the flux and reflux of the crowd, disorganized by these irregular movements, is pushed partly into the street, and partly into the warehouse on the second story, amid oaths, imprecations, and peals of laughter; while their discomfiture is hailed, with added uproar, by the drinkers already established in the wine-shops of the ground floor, in defiance of the sage counsels of the monks.

From one room to another, among tables covered with dishes, and surrounded with guests, are seen circulating the hostess and *giannine*, or waitresses of the house; some with gay-coloured aprons, powdered hair, and the coquettish little poniard, which forms part of their holiday costume; others with short petticoats, long braids of hair, naked feet, and a thousand glittering ornaments of tinsel or gold.

But to these animated scenes in the village or the road,—the chamber or the street,—to these cries, songs, exclamations, the noise of music, dancing, talking, and the jingling of plates and glasses, other sounds of a different nature are about to succeed.

In an hour the thundering noise of cannon will be heard; cannon almost harmless, indeed, and likely only to break the windows of the houses. The little street will echo with the word of command, and every house be eclipsed by the smoke of volleys of musketry, charged with powder. Then, beware of pillage, unless every remnant of provision has been placed in safety; nay, let the gay *giannina* look to herself: for a mimic war is apt, in such particulars, to imitate its prototype. In great particulars, however, no less: for nothing can exceed the majesty of the preparations for the sham-fight upon the plain of Marengo.

A magnificent throne, planted round with tri-coloured standards, is raised upon one of the few hillocks which diversify the field. Already the troops, in every variety of uniform, are defiling towards the spot. The trumpet appeals to the cavalry; the rolling of drums seems to cover the whole surface of the plain, which trembles under the heavy progress of the artillery and ammunition-wagons. The aide-de-camps, in their glittering uniforms, are galloping hither and thither; the banners waving to the wind, which causes, at the same time, a pleasing undulation of the feathers, aigrettes, and tri-coloured plumes; while the sun, that ever-present guest at the fêtes of Napoleon, that radiant illustrator of the pomps and vanities of the empire, casts its vivid reflections upon the golden embroideries, the brass and bronze of the cannon, helmets, cuirasses, and the sixty thousand bayonets bristling the tumultuous field.

By degrees, the troops, arriving with hurried march at the appointed spot, continue to force backward, in a wild semi-circle of retreat, the crowds of curious spectators, broken up like the rippling billows of the ocean, by the progress of one enormous wave; while a few horsemen charging along the line, proceed to clear the field for action.

The village is now deserted; the gay tents are struck, the trestles removed, the songs and clamours reduced to silence. On all sides are to be seen, scattered along the vast circuit of the plain, men interrupted in their sport or repast, and women dragging away their children, terrified by the flashing sabres, or loud neighing of the chargers.

It is no difficult matter to discern, by attentively examining the countenances of the men still collected under the same colours, to *which* among them the orders of the general-in-chief, Marshal Lannes, has assigned, in the coming fray, the glory of victory,— to *which* the duty of being vanquished; while the gallant marshal himself, followed by a numerous *état major*, is seen tracing and reconnoitring the ground, on which it has been already his lot to figure with such distinction. He now distributed to each brigade its part in the coming battle; taking care, however, to omit in the representation, the blunders of that great and terrible day, the 14th of June, 1800: for, after all, it is but a delicate flattery in military tactics, a madrigal, composed with salvos of artillery, which is about to be recited in honour of the new sovereign of Italy.

The troops now proceed to form into line, deploy, and form again, at the word of command; when military symphonies are heard from the side of Alexandria; vague murmurs increase from the mass of human population, which, protected by the streams of the Tanaro, the Bormida, the Orba, and the ravines of Tortona, form the moving girdle of the vast arena. Suddenly, the drums beat to arms; cries and huzzas burst from amid circling clouds of dust; sabres glitter in the sunshine; muskets are shouldered, as if by a mechanical movement; while a brilliant equipage, drawn by eight noble horses, caparisoned and emblazoned with the arms of Italy and France, conveys to the foot of their throne, the Emperor and Empress—Napoleon and Josephine.

The Emperor, after receiving homage from all the deputations of Italy, the envoys of Lucca, Genoa, Florence, Rome, and even

Prussia, mounts impatiently on horseback; and, instantaneously, the whole plain is overspread with fire and smoke.

Such were the sports of the youthful hero! War for his pastime, war for the accomplishment of his puissant destinies! Nothing less than war could satisfy that ardent temperament, formed for conquest and supremacy, to which the subjugation of the whole world would alone have left an hour of leisure!

An officer, appointed by the Emperor, stood explaining to Josephine, as she sat solitary on her throne, half terrified by the spectacle before her, the meaning of the various manœuvres, and the object of every evolution. He showed her the Austrian general, Melas, expelling the French from the village of Marengo, overpowering them at Pietra-Buona, at Castel-Ceriola; and Bonaparte suddenly arresting him in the midst of his victorious career, with only nine hundred men of the consular guard. Her attention was next directed to one of the most important movements of the battle.

The republicans appear to be giving way, when Desaix suddenly appears on the Tortona road; and the terrible Hungarian column, under Zach, marches to meet him. But, while the officer was yet speaking, Josephine's attention is diverted from the military movements, by a sort of confusion around her; on demanding the cause of which, she is informed that "a young girl, having imprudently cleared the line of military operations, at the risk of being crushed by the artillery, or trampled by charges of cavalry, is creating farther confusion by her obstinacy in pressing towards the presence of her majesty, the Empress-Queen."

CHAPTER II.

TERESA, for the intruder was no other than the daughter of Girardi, had been for a moment overcome by the intelligence she received at Turin of the departure of the Emperor for Alexandria. But it was fatigue rather than discouragement which made her pause; and nothing but the recollection that an unhappy captive was dependent upon her for the accomplishment of his only wish on earth, would have urged her forward upon her perilous errand. Without regard, therefore, to her weariness or loss of time, she signified to the guide her intention of proceeding at once to Alexandria.

"*To Alexandria!* 'Tis twice as far as we have come already!" cried the man.

"No matter, we must set out again immediately."

"I, for my part, shall not set out again before to-morrow," replied the guide; "and then, only to return to Fenestrella; so a pleasant journey to you, signora!"

All the arguments she could use, were unavailing to change his determination. The man, who had enveloped himself in the iron obstinacy of the Piedmontese character, speedily unsaddled his horses, and laid himself down between them in the stable, for a good night's rest.

But Teresa, firmly devoted to her enterprise, would not now recede from the undertaking. Having made up her mind to pursue her journey, she entreated the landlady of the inn in the *Dora Grossa*, where she had put up, to procure her the means of proceeding to Alexandria without a moment's delay; and the hostess instantly despatched her waiters in various directions through the city in search of a conveyance; but without success! From the Suza gate to that of the Po, from the Porta Nuova to that of the palace, not a horse, carriage nor cart, public or private, was to be seen; all had long been engaged, in consequence of the approaching solemnization at Alexandria.

Teresa now gave herself up to despair! Absorbed in anxious thought, she stationed herself with downcast looks on the steps of the inn, where luckily the gathering darkness secured her from recognition by the inhabitants of her native city, when suddenly, the sound of approaching wheels became audible, accompanied by the tinkling of mule-bells; and at the very door where she was standing, there appeared two powerful mules drawing one of those long caravans in use among travelling merchants; of which the boxes, closed by heavy padlocks, are made to open and form a movable shop; but the only accommodation of which, for passengers, consists in a narrow leathern seat in front, half under cover of a small awning of oil-cloth.

The man and woman, owners of the cart and its merchandise, having alighted, began to stretch their arms and yawn aloud; stamping with their feet by way of rousing themselves after a long and heavy slumber. At length, having familiarly saluted the hostess, they took refuge in the chimney-corner, holding out their hands and feet towards the vine-stocks blazing on the hearth; and after ordering the mules to be unharnessed and carefully attended to, they began to congratulate each other on the conclusion of their tedious journey, ordered supper, and talked of bed

The hostess, too, was preparing for rest. The yawning waiters closed up the doors and window-shutters; and poor Teresa, watching with tearful eyes all these preparations, thought only of the hours that were passing away, the dying flower, and the despair of the Count de Charney.

"A night, a whole night!" she exclaimed; "a night of which every minute will be counted by that unhappy man; while *I* shall be safe asleep. Nay, even to-morrow, it will be perhaps impossible for me to find a conveyance!"

And she cast her wistful eyes upon the two travellers, as if her last hope lay in their assistance. But she was still ignorant of the road they were to take, or whether they could or would be troubled with her company; and the poor girl, unaccustomed to find herself alone among strangers, still less among strangers of such a class, impelled by anxiety, but withheld by timidity, advanced a step towards them, then paused, mute, trembling, and undecided; when she was startled by the approach of a female servant, holding a candle and a key, who pointed out to her the room into which she was to retire for the night. Forced by this proposition to take some immediate step, Teresa put aside the arm of the *giannina*, and advancing towards the couple, engaged in munching their supper, entreated pardon for the interruption, and inquired what road they were to take on quitting Turin.

"To Alexandria, my pretty maid," replied the woman, starting at the question.

"To Alexandria! 'Twas then my guardian angel who brought you hither!" cried Teresa, overjoyed.

"I wish he had picked out a better road, then, signorina," cried the woman, "for we are all but ground to powder!"

"But what do you want with us? How can we serve you?" interrupted the man.

"Urgent business carries me to Alexandria. Can you give me a cast?" inquired Teresa.

"Out of the question," said the wife.

"I will pay you handsomely; two pieces of St. John the Baptist; that is, ten livres of France."

"I don't know how we could manage it," observed the man. "In the first place, the bench is so narrow that it will be scarcely possible to sit three; though I own, signorina, 'tis no great matter of room you will take up. In the next place, we are going only as far as the *Mercato* of Renigano, near Asti, which is only half-way to Alexandria."

"No matter," cried Teresa; "convey me only so far as to the gates of Asti. But we must set out this very night — this very moment."

"Impossible! quite impossible!" exclaimed both husband and wife at the same moment. "We made no bargain of our night's rest."

"The sum shall be doubled," said Teresa, in a lower voice, 'if you will only oblige me."

The man and the woman interchanged looks of interrogation.

"No," cried the wife, at last; "we shall fall ill of fatigue on the road. Besides, Losca and Zoppa want rest. Do you wish to kill the poor mules?"

"Four pieces, remember!" murmured the husband. "Four pieces!"

"What is that to the value of Losca and Zoppa!"

"Double price, recollect, for only half the fare, and no danger to the beasts."

"Pho! pho! a single Venetian sequin is worth two *parpaiole* of Genoa."

Nevertheless, the notion of four crowns to be earned so easily was not without its charm for either wife or husband, and at last, after farther objections on one side, and supplications on the other, the mules were brought out and re-harnessed. Teresa, enveloped in her mantle, to protect her from the night air, arranged herself as well as she could on the bench between the grumbling couple; and at length they set off on their expedition. All the clocks in Turin were striking eleven as they passed the gate of the city.

In her impatience to arrive and procure good tidings for transmission to Fenestrella, Teresa would fain have found herself carried away by the speed of impetuous coursers towards Alexandria. But alas! the vehicle in which she had secured a place lumbered heavily along the road. The mules paced steadily along, lifting their legs with measured precision, so as to put in motion the little chime of bells, which imparted a still cooler character to the nonchalance of their movements. For some time, indeed, the fair traveller took patience, hoping the animals would become gradually excited, or that the driver might urge them with a touch of the whip. But finding his incitement limited to a slight clicking of the tongue, she at length took courage to inform him that it was essential to make all speed towards Asti, that she might arrive by day-break at Alexandria.

"Take my word for it, my pretty maid," replied the man, "that 'tis not a whit more amusing to us than to yourself, to pass the night in counting the stars. But the cobbler must stick to his last. My cargo, young lady, consists of crockery ware, which I am conveying for sale to the fair of Renigano, and if my mules were to take to the trot, I should have only potsherds to produce at the end of my journey."

"Are you, then, a crockery merchant?" exclaimed Teresa, in a tone of consternation.

"China merchants," remonstrated the wife.

"Alas! alas!" exclaimed the disappointed girl, — "is it then impossible for you to go a little faster?"

"Except by knocking to pieces my whole freight."

"It is so important for me to arrive in time at Alexandria!"

"And for us to keep an eye to our goods."

As an act of concession, however, he condescended to bestow a few additional clickings upon his beasts; but the mules were too well broken to their pace, to risk their master's property by quickening their speed.

Teresa now began to reproach herself with inconsideration, in not having acquainted herself with the length of time necessary to reach Asti, or personally attempted to discover in Turin some more expeditious mode of conveyance. But she had nothing now left for it but patience! The vehicle jogged on at its accustomed rate, Losca and Zoppa soon managed to take the soft sides of the road, avoiding the rough jumbling of the pavement; and at length, the merchant and his wife, after a few mutual consultations respecting their chance of success at the fair of Renigano, relapsed into silence; in the midst of which, soothed by the darkness, oppressed by the cold, and lulled by the monotonous tinkling of the mule-bells, Teresa was overpowered with drowsiness. Her head, which wandered in search of a resting-place from the shoulder of the driver to that of his wife, at length inclined heavily on her own bosom.

"Lean upon me, my poor child; and happy dreams to you!" said the man, in a compassionate tone; and having accepted his offer, the overwearied Teresa was soon in a deep sleep.

When she opened her eyes again, daylight was shining brightly upon her! Startled to find herself in the open air, on the high road, she strove to recall her bewildered recollections; and on attaining perfect consciousness, perceived with horror that the vehicle was standing still, and appeared to have been some time stationary. The merchant, his wife, the very mules were fast asleep; not the slightest sound proceeded from the chime of bells!

Teresa now perceived at some distance on the road they had been traversing, the pinnacles of several steeples; and through the fantastic grouping of the morning mists, fancied she could discern the heights of the Superga, the Château of Mille Fiori, the Vigna della Regina, the Church of the Capuchins, all the rich adornments of the noble hills overhanging Turin.

"Merciful Heaven!" vociferated the poor girl, — "we have scarcely got beyond the suburbs!"

Roused by this exclamation, the driver rubbed his eyes and hastened to reassure her. "We are approaching Asti," said he. "The steeples you see behind you are those of Renigano. No cause to find fault with Losca and Zoppa; they can only just have begun their nap. Poor beasts!—they have earned their rest hardly. Heaven send they may not have profited by mine, to make a trot of it. Teresa smiled. "Gee!—away with you, jades!" he continued, with a crack of the whip which awoke both his wife and the mules. And soon afterwards, at the gates of Asti, the worthy china-man took leave of his passenger, assisted her to alight, and after signing the cross over the twenty livres he received for her fare, turned straight round with his mules, and made off deliberately for Renigano.

Half of her way to Alexandria was thus accomplished; but, alas! it was now scarcely possible to arrive in time for the levee of the Emperor. "Yet no doubt an Emperor must be late in rising!" thought Teresa; and oh! how she longed to thrust below the horizon again the sun which was just making its importunate appearance! Expecting that every thing around her would bear tokens of her own agitation, she fancied the whole population of Asti must be already astir, in preparation for a journey to Alexandria; and that amid the confusion of carriages and carts about to take the road, it would be easy to secure a place in some public conveyance.

What, therefore, was her astonishment; on entering the town, to find the streets still silent and deserted; and the sun scarcely yet high enough to shine on more than the roofs of the highest houses and the dome of the church! It occurred to her at that moment, that one of her maternal relations resided at Asti, who might render her assistance; and perceiving through the ground-floor window of a mean-looking house, the red glimmering of a fire, she knocked and ventured to inquire her way to the abode of her kinsman. A harsh voice answered her through the window that, for the last three months, the individual in question had been residing at his country-house at Monbercello; and thus disappointed, and alone in the solitary streets of a strange town, Teresa began to feel terrified and uneasy. To reanimate her courage, she turned towards a Madonna, before which, in an adjoining niche, a lamp was burning, and breathed her morning prayer. Scarcely had she concluded her orisons, when she was startled by the sound of approaching footsteps, and a man soon made his appearance.

"Can you tell me of a conveyance to Alexandria?" said she, civilly accosting the stranger.

"Too late, my pretty one! every cart and carriage has been bespoken this week past!" he replied, and hastened on his way.

A second man came by, to whom Teresa ventured to address the same inquiry. But this time, the answer was delivered in a harsh and reproving tone.

"You want to be running after the French, then, *razza male, detta?*" cried he; making off after his companion.

Teresa stood silent and intimidated at the accusation. At last, perceiving a young workman singing as he proceeded gaily to his business, she ventured to renew her inquiries.

"Aha, signorina!" cried he, in a tone of bantering, "you must needs make one in the battle, eh? But there will be little room left yonder for pretty damsels; better stay with us here, at Asti. 'Tis a fête to-day. The dancing will begin early in the afternoon; and the *drudi ballarini* will fall to breaking each other's heads, to have you for a partner. Faith, you are worth the trouble of a fight! Eh! what say you to a skirmish in your honour?"

And, approaching Teresa Girardi, he was about to throw his arm round her waist; but, startled by her indignant glance and exclamation, desisted, and resumed his song and his occupation.

A fourth, a fifth, now traversed the street, but the poor girl no longer hazarded an inquiry; but kept watching every opening door, and peeping into every courtyard in hopes to find some carriage in waiting. At length, by especial favour, she managed to obtain a place as far as Annone. Between Annone and Felizano — between Felizano and Alexandria — she was perplexed by a thousand farther difficulties. But with courage and perseverance, all were at length surmounted, and she arrived happily at Alexandria. As she anticipated, the Emperor had already taken his departure for Marengo; and without pausing a moment for deliberation, she followed the crowd which was pouring from the suburbs along the road towards the field of battle.

Hurried on with the multitude, pressed and jostled on all sides, watching eagerly for openings in the crowd, skirting the outermost edges of the road, Teresa neglected no opportunity of pushing forward. Undisturbed by the clamour of the trumpets, the sports of the merry-andrews, or the discourses of the monks, she pursued her way in the midst of the laughing, yelling, shouting populace, which went leaping on in the heat and dust; — a poor solitary stranger, apart from the sports and the joys of the day, — her countenance anxious, — her eye haggard, — and raising her hand at intervals to wipe away the dew from her weary brows.

But the whole force and fortitude of Teresa's mind were devoted to her progress. She has scarcely even found a moment for the contemplation of the farther means to be adopted. But a halt being suddenly imposed upon the crowd on reaching the outskirts of the field, she began to reflect on the uneasiness the prolongation of her absence would cause to her father (since the guide who had deserted her at Turin would not be permitted to enter the prison). She thought of Charney accusing his messenger of neglect and indifference; then felt for the petition in her bosom, apprehensive that, by some unlucky chance, it might have escaped her.

At the idea of her father grieving over the unwonted absence of his child, tears rushed into the eyes of Teresa; and it was from a reverie produced by these painful emotions, that she was recalled to herself by the cries of joy bursting from the surrounding multitude. An open space had been formed just beside the spot where she was resting, around which the crowd seemed circling; and the moment Teresa turned her head to ascertain the cause of the tumult, her hands were seized, and in spite of her resistance, her depression, her fatigue, she found herself compelled to take part in a *farandola*, which went whirling along the road, recruiting all the pretty girls and sprightly lads who could be involved in the diversion.

Vexatious as was the interruption, Teresa at length found means to disengage herself from such unsatisfactory society; and having contrived by a painful effort to push her way through the crowd, she at length obtained a glimpse of the vast plain glittering with troops; and her eyes having wandered for some minutes over the splendid army, paused upon the little hillock occupied by the imperial court. At the sight of the throne, the aim and end of her perilous journey, Teresa's heart leaped for joy; her courage returned, her strength seemed renewed. All her preceding cares were forgotten. But how to attain the wished-for spot? How to traverse those battalions of men and horses? There was madness in the very project!

But that which at first sight presented an obstacle, soon appeared to farther her intentions. The foremost ranks of the crowd pouring in torrents from Alexandria, having deployed to the right and left, on reaching the plain, were gradually gaining the banks of the Tanaro and the Bormida; where, at one moment, they pushed on so impetuously as to seem on the point of taking possession of the field of battle. A small body of cavalry instantly galloped towards the spot, waving their naked sabres, and by the plunging of their chargers causing the terrified crowd to return to the limits assigned them. The intruders evacuated the territory as rapidly as they had gained it, with the exception of a single individual:—that individual was Teresa Girardi!

In an adjacent hollow of the plain, surrounded by a strong quickset hedge, and sheltered by a small thicket of trees, flowed a spring of limpid water; towards which, thrust onwards by the crowd of spectators, the poor girl, whose eyes were fixed upon the throne in the distance, found herself irresistibly impelled. Apprehensive every moment of being crushed in the throng, she seized in her arms the trunk of the nearest poplar tree; and closing her eyes, like a child who fancies the danger has ceased to exist which it is not obliged to look upon,—remained motionless, her hearing confused by the rustling of the surrounding foliage

The advance and retreat of the mob was, in fact, so instantaneous, that when Teresa re-opened her eyes, she was quite alone, separated from the troops by the hedge and thicket, and from the crowd by a column of dust, produced by the last detachment of fugitives. Throwing herself at once into the little copse, she found herself in the centre of about twenty poplar and aspen trees, overshadowing a crystal spring, welling out of the ground over a bed of ivy, moss and celandine, till, bubbling onward in a silver thread, it gradually formed a brook capable of traversing the plain, over which its course was defined by painted tufts of blue forget-me-not, and the clusters of the white ranunculus. The refreshing exhalations of the shady spot assisted to restore the self-possession and strength of the exhausted girl. Teresa felt as though she had reached an oasis of verdure in the desert, sheltered from dust, and heat, and disturbance.

Meanwhile the plain has become suddenly quiet; she hears neither the word of command, the huzza of the crowd, nor the neighing of the horses. All she can discern is a singular movement overhead; and, looking up, Teresa perceives every bough and spray of the trees to be covered with flights of sparrows, driven to shelter from all quarters of the plain by the alarming movement of the troops and the incursions of the crowd. The poor birds, like the poor girl contemplating them, have taken refuge in that verdant solitude, their little wings and throats apparently paralysed by affright; for not a sound breaks from the band of feathered fugitives. Even on the advance of a brigade of cavalry towards the thicket, accompanied by the braying of trumpets, not a bird is seen to stir. They appear to wait anxiously for the result; while a similar feeling prompts Girardi's daughter to look through the foliage upon the field.

Her eyes are quickly attracted by files of troops, which appear to have cut off all communication between the thicket and the road.

"After all," thought the trembling Teresa, "it is but a *sham-fight* that is about to take place; and if I have been imprudent in venturing hither, the Almighty, who knows the innocence of my heart, will keep me in time of trouble!"

And, directing her attention through the opposite extremity of the thicket, she discerns, at the distance of about three hundred paces, the throne of Josephine and Napoleon. The space between, is occupied by the manœuvres of the soldiers; but every now and then, the ground is sufficiently cleared to admit of passing. Teresa now takes courage!—she feels that a decisive moment is at hand. Having opened a way through the hedge, she is about to advance, when the disorder of her toilet suddenly occurring to her mind, brings blushes into her cheeks. Her tresses, unbraided and dishevelled, are floating over her shoulders; her hands, her face, her person, are disfigured with dust. To present herself in such a condition before the sovereigns of Italy and France, were perhaps to insure her rejection, and the failure of her anxious mission.

Re-entering the thicket, therefore, and drawing near to the spring, she unties her large Leghorn hat, shakes out and smooths down her raven hair, braids up the flowing tresses, bathes her hands and face; and, having completed her morning toilet, breathes a prayer to Heaven for its blessing upon the merciful purpose which has cast her, thus defenceless, into the ranks of an army.

While watching for an auspicious moment to recommence her course, the stunning detonations of the cannon roar, from twenty different points, into her ears. The ground seems to tremble under her feet; and, while the poor girl stands motionless with consternation, the scared birds, fluttering from the trees above, with discordant cries and bewildered wings, make off for the woods of Valpedo and Voghera.

The fight has begun! Teresa, deafened by the roar of artillery and the universal clamour, stands transfixed, gazing towards the throne, which is sometimes concealed from her by clouds of smoke; sometimes by a screen of lances or bayonets.

After the lapse of half an hour, during which every idea seemed to abandon her mind, but that of indescribable terror, the energy of her soul resumed its force. She examined, with greater composure, the obstacles with which she is beset; and decided that it may still be possible to attain the imperial throne. Two columns of infantry, prolonged into a double line, to which the flanks of the thicket form a centre, were beginning to engage in an animated fire upon each other. Under cover of the clouds of smoke, she trusted to make her way between them, unobserved. Still, however, Teresa trembled at the attempt, when a troop of hussars, burning with thirst, suddenly invaded her asylum, and the maiden hesitated no longer. Her courage was roused, the moment her modesty took the alarm. She rushed forth at once between two columns of infantry; and when the smoke began to subside, the soldiers raised a cry of astonishment, on perceiving in the midst of them, the white dress and straw hat of a young girl,—a young and pretty Piedmontese,—whom each made it his immediate business to capture.

At that moment, a squadron of cuirassiers was galloping up to re-enforce one of the lines; the captain of which was on the point of trampling down the unfortunate Teresa; but, pulling up his horse in time, he gave her in charge to two soldiers of the line; not, however, without a few oaths and great wonder at such a apparition on the field of battle.

One of the two cuirassiers deputed to escort her to quarters, quickly raised her to his saddle; and it was thus she was conveyed to the rear of the hillock, where a few ladies belonging to the suite of the Empress were stationed, accompanied by an aid-de-camp and the *corps diplomatique* of the Italian deputations.

Teresa now fancied that her enterprise was accomplished. She had surmounted too many difficulties to be discouraged by the few remaining; and when, on her demand to be admitted to the Emperor, she was informed that he was on the field, at the head of the troops, she entreated an audience of the Empress. But this request appeared no less inadmissible than the other. To get rid of her importunities, the by-standers had recourse to intimidation, and Teresa's courage rose against their efforts. They insisted that she should at least wait the conclusion of the evolutions; and were astonished to find her persist in forcing her way towards the throne. Detained and threatened, her struggles became the more vehement. It was then that, raising her voice in self-defence, its piteous accents reached the ear of Josephine, to which the voice of a female in distress and appealing to her protection, were never known to be addressed in vain.

CHAPTER III.

SCARCELY were the commands of the Empress issued that no farther obstruction should be offered to the young stranger, when the brilliant crowd opened, to yield a passage to Teresa Girardi, who appeared in the midst of the throng, in a suppliant attitude, as if scarcely aware of being released from the detention of her captors.

But on a sign from Josephine—a gracious sign, instantly recognised by those around as a token of indulgence—the young Piedmontese was set at liberty; and, on finding herself free, Teresa rushed to the foot of the throne, breathless with agitation, and, bending low before the Empress, proceeded to unfold a handkerchief which she had taken from her bosom.

"A poor prisoner, madam," said she, "implores the clemency of your majesty." But, with every disposition to indulgence, it was impossible for the Empress to divine the meaning of the strange-looking handkerchief which Teresa Girardi, sinking on one knee, tendered to her hands.

"Have you a petition to present to me?" demanded Josephine at last, of the trembling girl, in a tone of encouragement.

"*This*, madam, is a petition; this is the memorial of an unfortunate captive!" persisted Teresa, still holding up the handkerchief. But tears of terror and anxiety, flowing down her cheeks, almost concealed the smile which the gracious affability of the Empress had for a moment called into existence.

"Rise, my poor girl, rise!" said Josephine, in a tone of compassion. "You appear deeply interested in the welfare of the petitioner!"

Teresa blushed, and hung down her head. "I have never even spoken to him, madam," she replied: "but he is so deserving of pity! If your majesty would deign to read the statement of his misfortunes—"

Josephine now unfolded the handkerchief, touched to the heart by the evidence of misery and destitution conveyed in such a substitute for writing-paper. Pausing, however, after she had perused the first line of the petition, she exclaimed, "But this is addressed to the emperor!"

"And are you not his wife?" cried Teresa. "Deign, deign to read on! Every moment is of consequence. Indeed, there is no time to be lost!"

The fight was now at the hottest. The Hungarian column,

though exposed to the severe fire of Marmont's artillery, was formidable in its movements: Zach and Dessaix were face to face, and the result of their encounter was to decide the destinies of the battle. The cannonade became general: the field seemed to vomit flames and smoke; while the clamour of the soldiers, uniting with the clang of arms, and call of trumpets, agitated the air like a tempest. And it was while all this was proceeding around her, that the Empress attempted to give her attention to the following lines:—

"Sire—

"The removal of two stones from the pavement of the court of my prison will scarcely shake the foundation of your empire; and such is the favour I presume to ask of your majesty. It is not for myself I appeal to your protection. But in the stony desert in which I am expiating my offences against your government, a single living thing has solaced my sufferings, and shed a charm over my gloomy existence! A plant—a flower springing spontaneously among the stones of Fenestrella, is the object of my solicitude. Let not your majesty accuse me of folly—of madness; it needs to have been a prisoner, to appreciate the value of such a friend. To this poor flower am I indebted for discoveries which have dispelled the mists of error from my eyes, for my restoration to reason, for my peace of mind, nay, for my very life! It is dear to me, sire, as glory to yourself.

"Yet, at this moment, my precious plant is perishing before my eyes, for want of a little space for the expansion of its roots; and the Commandant of Fenestrella would fain submit to the Governor of Turin my petition for the removal of the two miserable stones that impede its growth. By the time that wisdom has decided the question, the plant will be dead; and it is therefore to your compassion, sire, I appeal for the preservation of my plant. Issue orders that may yet preserve it from destruction, and myself from despair.—I implore it on my bended knees; and should you deign to favour my suit, the benefit vouchsafed by your majesty shall be recorded in the inmost depths of my heart!

"I admit, sire, that this poor plant has softened the vengeance doomed by your majesty to fall upon my devoted head; but it has also subdued my pride, and cast me a suppliant at your feet. From the height of your double throne, deign, therefore, to extend a pitying glance towards us. It is not for your majesty to appreciate the power exercised by solitary confinement over even the strongest heart, the most iron fortitude. I do not complain of my captivity; I support my sentence with resignation. Be its duration as that of my own life; but spare, oh, spare my plant!

"The favour I thus presume to implore, must be conceded,

sire, on the spot, without the delay of a single hour! On the brow of the human criminal, justice may hold her sword suspended, in order to enhance the after-sentence of pardon; but nature's laws are more prompt in their operation. Delay but a single day, and even the mighty power of your majesty will be unavailing to farther the petition of the prisoner of Fenestrella.

"CHARNEY."

At that instant, a sudden discharge of artillery seemed to rend asunder the atmosphere, and immediately the thick smoke, cut into circles and lozenges by the thousand lightnings of the discharge, seemed to cover the field with a network of light and shade. But on the cessation of the firing, the curtain of smoke seemed gradually drawn aside; and a brilliant spectacle was given to view, sparkling under the radiance of the sun,—even that noble charge, in the original of which Desaix lost his life. Zach and his Hungarians, repulsed in front by Bondet, harassed on the left flank by the cavalry of Kellermann, were already thrown into disorder: after which, the intrepid consul, re-establishing his line of battle from Castel-Ceriola to St. Julian, resumed the offensive, overthrew the imperialists at every point, and forced Melas to a speedy retreat.

This sudden change of position, these grand movements of the army, this flux and reflux of the human tide, at the command of a single voice, the voice of a chief, motionless and calm in the midst of the general disorder, might have sufficed to produce an impression on the coldest imagination. From the groups surrounding the throne, accordingly, burst cries of triumph, and exulting acclamations; when the Empress, startled by the contrast afforded by these "vivats" to the hoarse uproar of the battle-field, was instantly roused from her reverie to a sense of what was passing around her. For to all those brilliant manœuvres and imposing spectacles, the future Queen of Italy had remained insensible; her feelings and looks alike preoccupied by the extraordinary memorial that still fluttered in her hand.

Teresa Girardi, meanwhile, attentive to every gesture of the Empress, felt instantaneously reassured by the soft smile of sympathy which overspread the countenance of Josephine while perusing the petition. With a beating heart, she stooped to imprint a grateful kiss on the hand extended towards her, a hand how puissant amid all its fragile fairness, for on its slender finger glittered the nuptial ring of Napoleon!

Dismissed by this gracious movement from the presence of the Empress, Teresa now hastened towards the women's quarters: and as soon as the field of Marengo was cleared of its multitudes, proceeded to the nearest chapel, to tender to her sovereign protectress, the Holy Virgin, an offering of prayer and tears, the token of her heartfelt gratitude; for in the condescension of Josephine she fancied she had obtained a pledge for the eventual fulfilment of her wishes.

CHAPTER IV.

The sympathy of the Empress-Queen had been, in fact, warmly excited by the memorial of the captive of Fenestrella. Every word of the petition conveyed the most touching appeal to her feelings. Josephine herself was an almost idolatrous lover of flowers; as the permanent advantages derived in France from her liberal encouragement of botanical science and patronage of its professors, continue to attest. Escaping from the cares and splendours of sovereignty, often did the empress recede from the courtier throng, to watch the expansion of some rare exotic, in her fine conservatories at Malmaison. There was the favourite empire of Josephine! She loved the imperial purple of the rich cactus, at that period a splendid novelty to European eyes, better than the hues of the rich mantle adorning her throne; and the delicate fragrance of her clustering magnolias, proved more intoxicating than the soothing but fatal breath of courtly adulation. At Malmaison she reigned despotic over thousands of beauteous subjects, collected from all quarters of the globe. She knew them face by face, name by name;—was fond of disposing them in classes, castes, or regiments; and when some fresh subject presented itself for the first time at her levee, was able to interrogate the new-comer, so as to ascertain his family and connexions, and assign him an appropriate station in the community of which every brigade had its banner, and every banner a fitting standard-bearer.

Following the example of Napoleon, she respected the laws and customs of those she rendered tributary. Plants of all countries found their native soil and climate restored to them by her providence. Malmaison was a world in miniature; within whose circumscribed limits were to be found rocks and savannahs,—the soil of virgin forests and the sand of the desert,—banks of marl or clay,—lakes, cascades, and strands liable to inundation. From the heat of a tropical climate, you might fly to the refreshing coolness of the temperate zone; and in these varied specimens of atmosphere and soil, flourished, side by side, the various races of vegetative kind, divided only by green edges or an intrenchment of glass windows.

When Josephine held her field-days at Malmaison, the review

was indeed calculated to excite the tenderest associations. First in the ranks was the hydrangea, which had recently borrowed from her charming daughter its French name of Hortensia. Glory, too, found its reminiscences there, as well as maternal affection. Following the victories of Bonaparte, she contrived to reap her share in the plunder of conquered countries; and Italy and Egypt paid tribute to her triumphant parterres. Blooming in resplendent union at Malmaison were the soldanella of the Alps,—the violet of Parma,—the adonis of Castiglione,—the carnation of Lodi,— the willow and plane of Syria,—the cross of Malta,—the water-lily of the Nile,—the hibiscus of Palestine,—the rose of Damietta. Such were the conquests of Josephine: and of those, at least, France still retains the benefits!

But even in the midst of these treasures, Josephine still cultivated, by predilection, a plant reminding her of her days of happy childhood; that beautiful jasmine of Martinique, whose seeds, gathered and resown by her own hand, served to bring to her recollection not only the sports of girlhood and the roof of her fathers, but her earliest home of wedded love.

With such pursuits and attachments, how could she fail to appreciate the passion of the prisoner for his flower,—his only flower, —his only companion! The widow of Beauharnais was not always the happy and prosperous inmate of a consular or imperial palace. Josephine has herself tasted the bitterness of captivity; and the lesson is not thrown away.

Nor has she altogether forgotten the brilliant, successful, but proud and *insouciant* Count de Charney; formerly so contemptuous amid the pleasures of the world, and so incredulous in the existence of human affections. To what is she to attribute the singular change in his style and temper? What influence has sufficed to soften that haughty character? He, who once refused the homage of his knee to the Most High, now kneels to a human throne to supplicate in utmost humility for the preservation of a plant!

"The flower which has wrought so great a miracle," thought the Empress, with a smile, "deserves to be preserved from destruction!" And eager to accomplish her benevolent purpose, she grew impatient of the protraction of the fight, and would fain have put an end to the last evolutions, in order to hasten her measures in favour of her petitioner.

The moment Napoleon, surrounded by his generals, made his reappearance, exhausted by his exertions, and doubtless expecting compliments from her lips, the Empress presented the handkerchief to his astonished eyes,—exclaiming,—"An order from your hand, sire; an order for the commandant of Fenestrella! and an express to despatch it to the fortress!"

In the earnestness of her purpose, her voice assumed an imperial tone, and her eyes an expression of impatience, as if some new conquest were within reach, and it was *her* turn to assume command and authority. But after surveying her from head to foot with an air of surprise and dissatisfaction, the Emperor turned on his heel and passed on without a word. As if still reviewing his troops, he appeared only to be finishing his inspection by the last individual of the brigade.

Impelled by the force of habit, he next proceeded to examine the field of action, unmoistened indeed with blood, but covered with trophies of the early harvest, cut down by his victorious troops: — fields of corn and rice were trampled or hacked into chaff! In some spots, the earth itself was ploughed into deep channels by the manœuvres of the artillery; while here and there, were scattered the buff-leather gloves of the dragoons, broken plumes, or shreds of gold lace; — nay, even a few limping foot-soldiers and chargers, lamed in the affray, still encumbered the ground.

At one moment of the day, however, more serious consequences than these appeared imminent. The French soldiers appointed to occupy, as Austrians, the village of Marengo, resenting the part assigned them as beaten troops, had chosen to prolong their resistance beyond the period specified in the programme; and a violent struggle took place between them and their opponents. The two regiments happened to be irritated against each other by the jealousies of garrison rivalship; and mutual insults and challenges having been exchanged on the spot, bayonets were crossed in earnest between the two corps.

But for the immediate intervention of the general officers present, a terrible contest would have taken place; and the mimic fight become only too fatally a reality. With some difficulty, the troops were made to fraternise, by an exchange of gourds; and these being unluckily empty, in order to perfect the reconciliation, the cellars of the village were laid under contribution. Excess now succeeded to obstinacy, but a unanimous cry of "*Vive L'Empereur*" having been fortunately raised by the men, the whole breach of discipline was placed to the account of military enthusiasm; and, after twenty healths had been tossed off, the gallant Austrians consented to stagger defeated from the field; while the victorious French made their triumphal entry into Marengo, dancing the farandola, singing the Marseillaise, and mingling occasionally in their hurrahs, the now forbidden cry of "*Vive la République*." But their insubordination was now justly attributed to the enthusiasm of intemperance.

The troops having been formed once more into line, Napoleon proceeded to a distribution of crosses of honour among the old soldiers, who, five years before, had fought with him on that memorable spot. A few of the more eminent of the Cisalpine magistrates also received decorations on the field: after which, accompanied by Josephine, the Emperor laid the first stone of a monument, intended to perpetuate the victory of Marengo; and the ceremonies of the morning accomplished, the whole court, followed by the whole army, took their way back towards Alexandria.

All this time the destinies of Picciola remained undecided!

CHAPTER V.

To conclude the solemnities of the day, a public banquet was offered to the Emperor and Empress by the city of Alexandria, in the Town Hall, which was splendidly decorated for the occasion; after which, their majesties, wearied by their exertions, retired to pass the evening in one of the private apartments allotted to their use. The Emperor and Empress were now together, attended only by the secretary of the former; and, while dictating his despatches, Napoleon continued to pace the room, rubbing his hands with an air of satisfaction. Josephine, meanwhile, stood beguiling the time allotted by her lord to the duties of empire, by admiring, in one of the lofty mirrors of the saloon, the elegant coquetry of her own dress, and the splendour of the jewels in which she was arrayed.

After the departure of the secretary, the Emperor took his seat; and, while resting his elbow on a table covered with crimson velvet, richly fringed with gold, he fell into a train of reflection, announced by the expression of his countenance, of a highly agreeable nature. But the silence in which he was absorbed was far from satisfactory to Josephine. She felt that he had deported himself harshly towards her that morning, in the affair of the Fenestrella memorial. But she was beginning to perceive that she had been precipitate in pressing her request at an inauspicious moment; and promised herself to repair the injury she might have done her *protégé*, by referring, at a more convenient season, his petition to the Emperor. The happy moment, she fancied, was now arrived!

Seating herself at the table, exactly opposite to Napoleon, and resting, like himself, her chin upon her hand, she met his inquiring looks with a smile, and demanded the subject of his cogitations.

"Of what am I thinking?" replied the Emperor, in a cheerful tone—"that the imperial diadem is a very becoming ornament, and that I should have been much to blame if I had not added such a trinket to your majesty's casket."

The smiles of Josephine subsided as he spoke, while those of the Emperor brightened. He was fond of repressing those nervous tremors and evil auguries on the part of the Empress, naturally excited by the extraordinary change of condition which had elevated a simple subject to the imperial throne.

"Are you not better pleased to salute me Emperor than general?" he persisted, without noticing her serious looks.

"I am!—for the higher title endows you with the prerogative of mercy!" she replied; "and I have an appeal to make to your clemency."

It was now Napoleon's turn to relapse into gravity. Knitting his brows, he prepared himself sternly for resistance;—ever on the watch lest the influence of Josephine over his mind should beguile him into some culpable weakness in matters of state.

"How often have you promised me," said he, in a tone of severity, "to interfere no more with the course of public justice?—Do you suppose that the privilege of according pardon is assigned to sovereigns, that they may gratify the caprices of their private feelings?—Mercy should be exercised only to soften the too rigorous justice of the laws, or rectify the errors of public tribunals. To extend one's hand in continual acts of forgiveness, is wantonly to multiply and strengthen the ranks of the enemies of government."

"Nevertheless, sire," remonstrated Josephine, concealing with her handkerchief the tendency to mirth which she could scarcely repress, "you will certainly comply with the request I am about to make."

"I doubt it."

"And I persist in my opinion; for it is an act of justice rather than of clemency, I implore at your hands. I demand that two oppressors should be removed from the post they hold! Yes! sire,—let them be dismissed with ignominy;—let them be condemned, and discarded for ever from the service of your majesty!"

"How, Josephine!" cried Napoleon, "it is by *your* lips that for once I am instigated to severity? Have *you* become the advocate of punishment? Upon whom, pray, are you thus desirous to call down vengeance?"

"Upon two flagstones, sire, which are superfluous in the pavement of a courtyard!" replied the Empress, indulging, unrestrained, in the merriment she had so long found it difficult to repress.

"Two flagstones! are you making a jest of me?" cried Napoleon, in a severe tone, piqued at supposing himself treated with levity by his wife.

"Never was I more truly in earnest," replied Josephine, "for on the removal of these two stones depends the happiness of a suffering human being. Let me entreat your majesty's attention to a history that requires your utmost indulgence, both towards myself and its unfortunate object." And without farther circumlocution, she proceeded to acquaint him with the particulars of her singular interview with Teresa Girardi, and the devoted services of the poor girl towards a friendless prisoner, whose name she studiously kept concealed. While enlarging on the sufferings of the captive, on his passion for his plant, and the disinterestedness of his young and lovely advocate—all the natural eloquence of a humane and truly feminine heart flowed from her lips, and irradiated her speaking countenance.

Impressed by the animation of her gestures, a respondent smile played upon the lips of the Emperor; but that smile, alas! was an exclusive tribute to the attractions and excellencies of his wife!

CHAPTER VI.

During this tedious interval, the unhappy Charney was counting the hours, the minutes, the seconds, with the utmost impatience: he felt as if the minutest divisions of time were maliciously heaping themselves together, to weigh down the head of his devoted flower!

Two days had now elapsed. The messenger brought back no tidings; and even the venerable Girardi was growing uneasy, and beginning to deduce evil auguries from the absence of his daughter. Hitherto, however, he had not named his messenger to the Count; and, while trying to awaken hope in the heart of his companion, experienced the mortification of hearing accusations against the zeal and fidelity of the person to whom the mission had been intrusted. Girardi could no longer refrain from accusing himself in secret of having hazarded the safety of his child. "Teresa, my daughter, my dear daughter!" he exclaimed, amid the stillness of his gloomy chamber, "what—what has become of you?" And, lo! the third day came, and no Teresa made her appearance.

When the fourth arrived, Girardi had not strength to show himself at the window. Charney could not even catch a glimpse of his fellow-prisoner; but had he lent a more attentive ear, he might, perhaps, have overheard the supplications, broken by sobs, addressed to Heaven by the poor old man, for the safety of his only child. A dark veil of misery seemed suddenly to have overspread that little spot; where, but a short time before, in spite of the absence of liberty, cheerfulness and contentment diffused their enlivening sunshine.

The very plant was progressing rapidly to its last; and Charney found himself compelled to watch over the dying moments of his Picciola. He had now a double cause for affliction; a dread of losing the object of his attachment, and of having degraded himself by useless humiliation;—if he should have humbled himself in the dust, only to be repulsed from the footstool of the usurper.

As if the whole world were in a conspiracy against him, Ludovico, formerly so kind, so communicative, so genuine, seemed unwilling now to address to him a single word. Taciturn and morose, the gaoler came and went, passed through the court, or returned by the winding staircase, with his pipe in his mouth, as if to avoid uttering a syllable. He seemed to have taken a spite against the affliction of his captive. The fact was, that from the moment the refusal of the commandant had been made known, the gaoler began to prepare for the moment which he foresaw was about to take place before him, the alternative of his duty and his inclination. Duty, he knew, must eventually prevail; and he affected sullenness and brutality, by way of gaining courage for the effort. Such is the custom of persons unrefined by the polish of education. In fulfilling whatever harsh functions may be assigned them, they try to extinguish every generous impulse in their souls, rather than soften them by courtesy of deportment. Poor Ludovico's goodness of heart was rarely demonstrated in *words;* and where kindly *deeds* were interdicted by those in authority over him, his secret compassion usually found vent in surliness towards the very victim exciting his commiseration. If his ill-humour should call forth resentment, so much the better: his duty became all the easier. War is indispensable between victim and executioner,—prisoner and gaoler.

When the dinner hour arrived, Ludovico, finding Charney transfixed in mournful contemplation beside his plant, took care not to present himself in the gay mood with which he was wont to accost the Count; sometimes sportively addressing his goddaughter as "*Giovanetta, fanciuletta,*" or inquiring after the health of the "Count and Countess;" but, traversing the court in haste, without noticing his prisoner, he pretends to suppose him in the chamber above. By some accidental movement, however, on the part of Charney, Ludovico suddenly found himself face to face with the captive; and was shocked to perceive the change which the lapse of a few days had effected in his countenance. Impatience and anxiety had furrowed his brow, and discoloured his lips, and wasted his cheeks; while the disorder of his hair and beard served to increase the wildness of his aspect. Against his will, Ludovico stood motionless, contemplating these melancholy changes; but, suddenly, calling to mind his previous resolutions, he cast an eye upon the flower, winked ironically, shrugged his shoulders, whistled a lively air, and was about to take his departure, when Charney murmured, in a scarcely recognisable voice, " What injury have I done to you, Ludovico?"

" *Me!*—done to *me!* None, that I know of," replied the gaoler, more deeply touched than he cared to show, by the plaintiveness of this apostrophe.

"In that case," said the Count, advancing towards him and seizing him by the hand, "be still my friend! Aid me while there is yet time! I have found means of evading all objections! The commandant can have no farther scruples,—nay, he need not know a word of the matter. Procure me only a box of earth, —we will gently raise the stones for a moment and transplant the flower—"

" 'Ta-ta-ta-ta-ta!" interrupted Ludovico, drawing back his hand. " The devil take the gilly-flower, for aught I care! She has done mischief enough already; beginning with yourself, who are about, I see, to have another fit of illness. Better make a pitcher of tisane of her before 'tis too late."

Charney replied by an eloquent glance of scorn and indignation.

" If it were only yourself who had to suffer," resumed Ludovico, " you would have yourself to thank, and there would be an end on't. But there is a poor old man, whom you have deprived of his daughter; for Signor Girardi will see no more of his unhappy Teresa."

" Deprived of his daughter!" cried the Count, his eyes dilating with horror, " how?—in what manner?"

"Ay! *how?* in what manner?" pursued the gaoler, setting down his basket of provisions, and taking the attitude of one about to administer a harsh reprimand. " People lay the whip to the horses, and pretend to wonder when the carriage rolls on. People let fly the stiletto, and pretend to wonder when blood flows from the wound. *Trondidio! O che frascheria!* You choose to write to the Emperor—'twas your own affair : you wrote. Well and good! You infringed the discipline of the prison, and the commandant will find 'tis time to punish you. Well and good again. But, because you must needs have a trusty messenger to convey your unlucky letter, nothing less would serve you than to employ the *povera damigella* on your fool's errand!"

"How!—you mean that Girardi's daughter—"

"Ay, ay! open your eyes, and look surprised," interrupted Ludovico. "Did you suppose that your correspondence with the Emperor was to be conveyed by the telegraph? The telegraph, sir, has got other business on hand. All that I have got to tell you is, that the commandant has discovered the whole plot; perhaps through the guide, (for the *Giovana* could not hazard herself alone on such an expedition.) And so she is forbid to re-enter the fortress. Her poor father will behold her face no more. And through whose fault, I should like to know?"

Charney covered his face with his hands, and groaned aloud.

"Unhappy Girardi! have I, indeed, deprived thee of thine only consolation?" cried he, at last. Then, turning to Ludovico, he inquired whether the old man was apprised of what had befallen him.

"He has known it since yesterday," replied the gaoler; "and no doubt loves you all the better. But make haste! your dinner is getting cold!"

Charney, overwhelmed with grief, sank upon his bench. A momentary pang suggested to him to crush Picciola at once, executing retributive justice upon her with his own hand. But he had not courage for a deed so ruthless; and a faint hope already seemed to glimmer in the distance, for his favourite. The young maiden, who had thus generously devoted herself to serve him, must be already returned. Perhaps she had been able to approach the Emperor? Yes! doubtless she has been admitted to the honour of an audience; and it is this discovery which has so irritated the commandant against her. The commandant may possibly have in his possession an order for the liberation of Picciola! In that case how dares he venture on further delay? The commands of the Emperor *must* be obeyed. Blessings, blessings," thought Charney, "on the noble girl who has befriended us—the girl whom I have been the means of separating from her father! Teresa! sweet Teresa! how willingly would I sacrifice half my existence for thy sake—for thy happiness—nay, what would I *not* give for the mere power of opening to thee once again the gates of the fortress of Fenestrella!"

CHAPTER VII.

Scarcely half an hour had elapsed after the intimation conveyed by Ludovico, when two municipal officers, arrayed in their tri-coloured scarfs of office, presented themselves, accompanied by the commandant, before the Count de Charney, and requested him to accompany them to his own chamber; on arriving in which, the commandant addressed his prisoner with considerable pomposity and deliberation.

The commandant was a man of dignified corpulency, having a round bald head, and gray and bushy whiskers. A deep scar, extending from his left eyebrow to the upper lip, seemed to divide his face in two. A long, blue, uniform coat, with prodigious skirts, buttoned closely to the chin, top-boots over his pantaloons, a slight tint of powder on his remnant of a braided pigtail, and scanty side-curls, spurs to his boots, (by way of distinction, doubtless, for the rheumatism had long constituted him chief prisoner in his own citadel;)—such were the outward and visible signs of the dignitary, whose only warlike weapon was the cane on which his gouty limbs leaned for support.

Appointed to the custody of prisoners of state alone, most of whom were members of families of distinction, the commandant piqued himself on his good breeding, in spite of frequent outbreaks of fury: and, in spite of certain infractions of prosody and syntax, on the chosen elegance of his language. He was upright, moreover, as a pikestaff; rejoiced in an emphatic and sonorous voice; flourished his hand when he attempted a bow, and scratched his head when he attempted a speech. Thus qualified and endowed, the brave Morand, captain and commandant of Fenestrella, passed for a fine soldierlike-looking man, and an efficient public functionary.

From the courteous tone assumed in his initiatory address, and the professional attitude of the two commissaries by whom he was accompanied, Charney fancied that their sole business was to deliver to him a reprieve for his unhappy Picciola. But the commandant's next sentence consisted in an inquiry, whether, upon any specific occasion, the prisoner had to complain of his want of courtesy or abuse of authority. The Count, still flattering himself that such a preamble augured well for the accomplishment of his hopes, certified all, and more than all, that civility seemed to require in reply to this leading question.

"You cannot, I imagine, sir, have forgotten," persisted the commandant, "the care and kindness lavished upon you during your illness? If it was not your pleasure to submit to the prescriptions of the physicians appointed to visit you, the fault was neither theirs nor mine, but your own. When it occurred to me that your convalescence might be accelerated by a greater facility for taking air and exercise, you were instantly allowed, at all times and seasons, access to the prison-court?"

Charney inclined his head in token of grateful affirmation. But impatience of the good man's circumlocution already caused him to compress his lips.

"Nevertheless, sir," resumed the commandant, in the tone of a man whose feelings have been wounded, and whose advances were repaid with ingratitude, "you have not scrupled to infringe the regulations of the fortress, of the tenor of which you could not have been ignorant; compromising me thereby in the eyes of General Menon, the governor of Piedmont; nay, perhaps, of his gracious majesty the Emperor himself. The memorial which you have contrived to place before him——"

"Place before him!" interrupted Charney; "has he then received it?"

"Of course he has received it."

"And the result—the result!" cried the Count, trembling with anxiety; "what has been decreed?"

"That, as a punishment for your breach of discipline, you are to be confined a month in the dungeon of the northern bastion of the fortress of Fenestrella."

"But what said the Emperor to my application?" cried the Count, unable to resign at once all his cherished hopes of redress.

"Do you suppose, sir, that the Emperor has leisure for the consideration of any such contemptible absurdities?" was the disdainful reply of the commandant; on which Charney, throwing himself in complete abstraction into the only chair the chamber happened to contain, became evidently unconscious of all that was passing around him.

"This is not all!" resumed the commandant; "your communications with the exterior of the fortress, being thus ascertained, it is natural to suppose that your correspondence may have been more extensive than we know of, and I beg to inquire whether you have addressed letters to any person besides his majesty the Emperor?"

To this address Charney vouchsafed no reply.

"An official examination of your chamber and effects is about to take place," added the man in authority. "These gentlemen are appointed by the governor of Turin for the inquisitorial duty, which they will discharge punctually, according to legal form, in your presence. But previous to the execution of the warrant, I request to know whether you have any personal revelations to make? Voluntary disclosures, sir, might operate favourably in your behalf."

Still, however, the prisoner remained obstinately silent; and the commandant, knitting his brows and contracting his high forehead into a hundred solemn wrinkles, assumed an air of severity, and motioned to the delegates of General Menon to proceed with their duty. They immediately began to ransack the chamber, from the

chimney and palliasse of the bed, to the linings of the coats of the prisoner; while Morand paced up and down the narrow chamber, tapping with his cane every square of the flooring, to ascertain whether excavations existed for the concealment of papers or preparations for flight. He called to mind the escape of Latude and other prisoners from the Bastille; where moats, both deep and wide, walls ten feet thick,—gratings, counterscarps, drawbridges, ramparts bristled with cannon and palisades, sentinels at every postern, on every parapet,—had proved insufficient to baffle the perseverance of a man armed with a cord and a nail! The Bastille of Fenestrella was far from possessing the same iron girdle of strength and security. Since the year 1796, the fortifications had been in part demolished, and the citadel was now defended only by a few sentries, planted on the external bastion.

After a search prolonged as far as the limited space would allow, nothing of a suspicious nature was brought to light, with the exception of a small vial, containing a blackish liquid, which had probably served the prisoner for ink. Interrogated as to the means by which it came into his possession, Charney turned towards the window, and began tapping with his fingers on the glass, without condescending to reply to the importunate querists.

The dressing-case still remained to be examined; but, on being required to give up the key, the Count, instead of presenting it with becoming respect to the commandant, almost threw it into the hand extended towards him.

Thus boldly defied in presence of his subordinates, the commandant disdained all farther attempts at conciliation. He was, in fact, suffocating with rage. His eyes sparkled, his complexion became livid, and he bustled up and down the little chamber, buttoning and unbuttoning his coat, as if to exhaust the transports of his repressed indignation.

At length, by a spontaneous movement, the two sbirri, occupied in the examination of the casket, holding it in one hand and turning over its contents with the other, advanced towards the window, to ascertain whether it contained secret drawers, and immediately exclaimed, in tones of triumph, "All's right! The mystery is in our hands."

Drawing out from beneath the false bottom of the case a number of cambric handkerchiefs, closely scribbled over and carefully folded, they were satisfied of having obtained possession of the proofs of a widely-organized conspiracy; for at this profanation of the sacred archives so dear to him, Charney started up and extended his hand to snatch back the treasures of which he saw himself despoiled. Then, struck by the consciousness of his own incapacity of resistance, he reseated himself in his chair, without uttering a syllable of remonstrance.

But the impetuosity of his first movements was not lost upon the governor; who saw at once that the documents which had fallen into his hands were of the highest importance in the estimation of the Count. The handkerchiefs, therefore, were deposited, on the spot, in a government despatch-bag, duly sealed and docketed. Even the soot-bottle and tooth-pick were confiscated to the state! A report was drawn up of the proceedings which had taken place, to which the signature of Charney was formally demanded, —impatiently refused,—and the refusal duly recorded at the end of the document; after which, the commandant issued his mandate for the immediate transfer of the prisoner to the northern bastion.

What vague, confused, and painful emotions prevailed, meanwhile, in the mind of the prisoner! Charney was alive only to a single stroke of his afflictions; a stroke which deadened his consciousness of all the rest. He had not so much as a smile of pity to bestow upon the imaginary triumph of the blockheads who were carrying off what they supposed to be the groundwork of a criminal impeachment; but which consisted in a series of scientific observations upon the growth and properties of his plant;—Yes; even his tenderest recollections snatched from his possession; and an impassioned lover required to give up the letters of his mistress, can alone enter into the despair of the captive. To preserve Picciola from destruction, he had tarnished his honour, his self-esteem; broken the heart of a benevolent old man: destroyed the happiness of a gentle and lovely girl; and of all that had sufficed to attach him to a life of wretchedness. Every trace is now effaced—every record destroyed—the very journal of those happy hours which he had enjoyed in the presence of his idol, is torn for ever from his possession!

CHAPTER VIII.

THE intervention of Josephine in Charney's favour had not proved so efficient as might have been supposed. At the conclusion of her mild intercessions in favour of the prisoner and his plant, when she proceeded to place in the hands of Napoleon the handkerchief inscribed with his memorial, the Emperor recalled to mind the singular indifference—so mortifying to his self-love—with which, during the warlike evolutions of the morning at Marengo, Josephine had cast her vacant, careless gaze upon the commemoration of his triumph. And thus predisposed to displeasure, the obnoxious name of Charney served only to aggravate his ill-humour.

"Is the man mad?" cried he, " or does he pretend to deceive me by a farce? A Jacobin turned botanist?—about as good a jest as Marat descanting in the tribune on the pleasures of a pastoral life; or Couthon presenting himself to the Convention with a rose in his button-hole!"

Josephine vainly attempted to appeal against the name of Jacobin thus lightly bestowed upon the Count; for, as she commenced her remonstrance, a chamberlain made his appearance to announce that the general officers, ambassadors, and deputies of Italy, were awaiting their majesties in the audience-chamber;—where, having hastily repaired, Napoleon immediately burst forth into a denunciation against visionaries, philosophers, and liberals, mainly inspired by the recent mention of the Count de Charney. In an imperious tone, he threatened that all such disturbers of public order should be speedily reduced to submission; but the loud and threatening tone he had assumed, which was supposed to be a spontaneous outbreak of passion, was, in fact, a premeditated lesson bestowed on the assembly; and more especially on the Prussian ambassador, who was present at the scene. Napoleon seized the opportunity to announce to the representatives of Europe the divorce of the Emperor of the French from the principles of the French revolution!

By way of homage to the throne, the subordinates of the Emperor hastened to emulate his new profession of faith. The general commandant at Turin, more especially, Jacques-Abdallah Menon, forgetting or renouncing his former principles, burst forth into a furious diatribe against the pseudo Brutuses of the clubs and taverns of Italy and France; on which signal arose from the minions of the empire a unanimous chorus of execrations against all conspirators, revolutionists, and more especially Jacobins; — till, overawed by their virulence, Josephine began to tremble at the storm she had been unwittingly the means of exciting. At length, drawing near to the ear of Napoleon, she took courage to whisper, in a tone of mingled tenderness and irony, — "What need, sire, of all these denunciations? — My memorial regards neither a Jacobin nor a conspirator; but simply a poor plant, whose plots against the safety of the empire should scarcely excite such vast tumults of consternation."

Napoleon shrugged his shoulders. "Can you suppose me the dupe of such absurd pretences?" he exclaimed. "This Charney is a man of high faculties and the most dangerous principles:— would you pass him upon me for a blockhead?—The flower, the pavement, the whole romance, is a mere pretext. The fellow is getting up a plan of escape! It must be looked to. Menon! let a careful eye be kept upon the movements of those imprisoned for political offences in the citadel of Fenestrella. One Charney has presumed to address to me a memorial. How did he manage to forward his petition otherwise than through the hands of the commandant? Is such the discipline kept up in the state-prisons of the empire?"

Again the Empress ventured to interpose in defence of her *protégé*.

"Enough, madam, enough of this man!" exclaimed the commander-in-chief; and discouraged and alarmed by the displeasure expressed in his words and looks, Josephine cast down her eyes and was silent from confusion. General Menon, on the other hand, mortified by the public rebuke of the Emperor, was not sparing in the reprimand despatched to the captain-commandant of the citadel of Fenestrella; who, in his turn, as we have seen, vented his vexation on the prisoners committed to his charge. Even Girardi, in addition to the cruel sentence of separation from his daughter, (who on arriving full of hopes at the gate of the fortress, was commanded to appear there no more,) had been subjected, like Charney, to a domiciliary visit; by which, however, nothing unsatisfactory was elicited.

But emotions more painful than those resulting from the forfeiture of his manuscripts, now awaited the Count: as he traversed the courtyard on his way to the bastion with the commandant and his two acolytes, Captain Morand, who had either passed without notice on his arrival, the fences and scaffolding surrounding the plant, or was now stimulated by the arrogant contumacy of Charney to an act of vengeance, paused to point out to Ludovico this glaring breach of prison-discipline manifested before his eyes.

"What is the meaning of all this rubbish?" cried he. "Is *such*, sir, the order you maintain in your department?"

"*That*, captain," replied the gaoler, in a half-hesitating, half-grumbling tone, drawing his pipe out of his mouth with one hand, and raising the other to his cap in a military salute—"*that*, under your favour, is the plant I told you of,—which is so good for the gout, and all sorts of disorders."

Then, letting fall his arm by an imperceptible movement, he replaced his pipe in its usual place.

"Death and the devil!" cried the captain, "if these gentlemen were allowed to have their own way, all the chambers and courts of the citadel might be made into gardens, menageries, or shops,—like so many stalls at a fair. Away with this weed at once, and every thing belonging to it!"

Ludovico turned his eyes alternately towards the captain, the Count, and the flower, and was about to interpose a word or two of expostulation.—"Silence!" cried the commandant; "silence, and do your duty."

Thus fiercely admonished, Ludovico held his peace; removing the pipe once more from his mouth, he extinguished it, shook out the dust, and deposited it on the edge of the wall while he proceeded to business. Deliberately laying aside his cap, his waistcoat, and rubbing his hands as if to gain courage for the job, he paused a moment, then suddenly, with a movement of anger, as if against himself or his chief, seized the haybands and matting, and dispersed them over the court. Next went the uprights which had supported them; which he tore up one after the other, broke over his knee, and threw the pieces on the pavement. His former tenderness for Picciola seemed suddenly converted into a fit of abhorrence.

Charney, meanwhile, stood motionless and stupefied, his eyes fixed wistfully upon the plant thus exposed to view, as if his looks could still afford protection to its helplessness. The day had been cool, the sky overclouded, and from the stem, which had rallied during the night, sprang several little healthy, verdant shoots. It seemed as though Picciola were collecting all her strength to die!

To die!—Picciola!—his own, his only!—the world cf his existence and his dreams, the pivot on which revolved his very life, to be reduced to nothingness! Midway in his aspirations towards a higher sphere, the flight of the poor captive, over whose head heaven has suspended its sentence of expiation, is to be suddenly arrested! How will he henceforward fill up the vacant moments of his leisure?—how satisfy the aching void in his own bosom? Picciola, the desert which thou didst people is about to become once more a solitary wilderness! No more visions, no more hopes, no more reminiscences, no more discoveries to inscribe, no farther objects of affection!—How narrow will his prison now appear — how oppressive its atmosphere — the atmosphere of a tomb,—the tomb of Picciola! The golden branch,—the sibylline divining rod, which sufficed to exorcise the evil spirits by which he was beset, will no longer protect him against himself! The sceptic—the disenchanted philosopher, must return to his former mood of incredulity, and bear once more the burden of his bitter thoughts, with no prospect before him but eternal extinction! No,—death were a thousand times preferable to such a destiny!

As these thoughts glanced through the mind of Charney, he beheld, at the little grated window, the shadow of the venerable Girardi. "Alas!" murmured the Count, "I have deprived him of all he had to live for; and he comes to triumph over my affliction,—to curse me—to deride me! And he is right; for what are sorrows such as mine compared to those I have heaped upon his revered head?"

Charney perceived the old man clasping the iron window-bars in his trembling hands; but dared not meet his eyes, and hazard an appeal to the forgiveness of the only human being of whose esteem he was ambitious. The Count dreaded to find that venerable countenance distorted by the expression of reproach or contempt; and when at length their glances met, he was touched to the soul by the look of tender compassion cast upon him by the unhappy father;—forgetful of his own sorrows in beholding those of his companion in misfortune. The only tears that had ever fallen from the eyes of the Count de Charney, started at that trying moment! But, consolatory as they were, he dried them hurriedly as they fell, in the dread of exposing his weakness to the contempt and misapprehension of the men by whom he was surrounded.

Among the spectators of this singular scene, the two sbirri alone remained indifferent to what was passing—staring vacantly at the prisoner, the old man, the commandant, and the gaoler; wondering what reference their emotions might bear to the supposed conspiracy, and nothing doubting that the mysterious plant, about to be dislodged, would prove to have been a cover to some momentous hiding-place.

Meanwhile, the fatal operations proceeded. Under the orders of the commandant, Ludovico was attempting to take up the rustic bench, which at first seemed to resist his feeble efforts.

"A mallet—take a mallet!" cried Captain Morand.

Ludovico obeyed; but the mallet fell from his hands.

"Death and the devil! how much longer am I to be kept waiting?" now vociferated the captain; and the gaoler immediately let fall a blow, under which the bench gave way in a moment. Mechanically, Ludovico bent down towards his god-daughter, which was now alone and undefended in the court; while the Count stood ghastly and overpowered, big drops of agony rising upon his brow.

"Why destroy it, sir; why destroy it?—you must perceive that the plant is about to die!"—he faltered, descending once more to the abject position of a suppliant. But the captain replied only by a glance of ironical compassion. It was now his turn to remain silent!

"Nay, then," cried Charney, in a sort of frenzy, "since it must needs be sacrificed, it shall die by no hand but mine!"

"I forbid you to touch it!" exclaimed the commandant; and, extending his cane before Charney, as if to create a barrier between the prisoner and his idol, he renewed his orders to Ludovico; who, seizing the stem, was about to uproot it from the earth.

The Count, startled into submission, stood like an image of despair.

Near the bottom of the stem, below the lowest branches, where the sap had got power to circulate, a single flower, fresh and brilliant, had just expanded!—Already, all the others were drooping, withered, on their stalks; but this single one retained its beauty, as yet uncrushed by the rude hand of the gaoler. Springing in the midst of a little tuft of leaves, whose verdure threw out in contrast the vivid colours of its petals, the flower seemed to turn imploringly towards its master. He even fancied its last perfumes were exhaling towards him; and, as the tears rose in his eyes, seemed to see the beloved object enlarge, disappear, and at last bloom out anew. The human being and the flower, so strangely attached to each other, were interchanging an eternal farewell!

If, at that moment, when so many human passions were called into action by the existence of an humble vegetable, a stranger could have entered, unprepared, the prison-court of Fenestrella, where the sky shed a sombre and saddening reflection, the aspect of the officers of justice, invested in their tri-coloured scarfs—of the commandant, issuing his ruthless orders in a tone of authority—would naturally have seemed to announce some frightful execution; of which Ludovico was the executioner, and Charney the victim, whose sentence of death had just been recited to him. And see, they come!—strangers *are* entering the court;—two strangers, the one, an aide-de-camp of General Menon, the other, a page of the Empress Josephine. The dust with which their uniforms were covered, attests with what speed they have performed their journey to the fortress; yet a minute more, and they had been too late!

At the noise produced by their arrival, Ludovico, raising his head, relaxed his grasp of Picciola, and confronted Charney face to face. Both the gaoler and the prisoner were pale as death!

The commandant had now received from the hands of the aide-de-camp an order, the perusal of which seemed to strike him with astonishment; but after taking a turn or two in the courtyard, to compare in his mind the order of to-day with that of the day preceding, he assumed a more courteous demeanour, and, approaching the Count de Charney, placed in his hands the missive of General Menon. Trembling with emotion, the prisoner read as follows:—

"His majesty, the Emperor and King, deputes me, sir, to inform you, that he grants the petition forwarded to him by the prisoner Charney, now under your custody in the fortress of Fenestrella, relative to a plant growing among the stones of one of its pavements. Such as are likely to be injurious to the flower must be instantly removed; for which purpose you are requested to consult the wishes and convenience of your prisoner."

"Long live the Emperor!" cried Ludovico.

"Long live the Emperor!" murmured another voice, which seemed to issue from the adjoining wall; and while all this was proceeding, the commandant stood leaning on his cane, by way of keeping himself in countenance; the two officers of justice, completely puzzled, were trying in vain to connect the new turn of affairs with the plot which their imagination had created; while the aide-de-camp and page, secretly wondered what could be the motive of the haste which had been so urgently recommended to them. The latter now addressed Charney, to inform him that the letter contained a postscript in the handwriting of the Empress; and the Count, turning over the page, read aloud as follows:

"I earnestly recommend Monsieur the Count de Charney to the good offices of Captain Morand; to whom I shall feel personally obliged for any acts of kindness by which he may be enabled to alleviate the situation of his prisoner. JOSEPHINE."

"Long live the Empress!" cried Ludovico. Charney said not a word. *His* feelings could not be satisfied with less than raising to his lips the precious signature of his benefactress. The letter, held for some minutes in silence before his eyes, served to conceal his face from the curiosity of the spectators.

BOOK III.

CHAPTER I.

THE commandant of Fenestrella was now unrelaxing in his courtesies towards the protégé of her majesty the Empress Queen. There was no further mention of a transfer to the northern bastion; and Charney was even authorized to reconstruct his fences for the defence of Picciola; who, feeble and delicate after her recent transplantation, had more than ever occasion for protection. So completely indeed had Captain Morand's irritation of feeling against the prisoner and plant subsided, that every morning Ludovico appeared with a message of inquiry from the commandant after the wants and wishes of the Count, and the health of his pretty Picciola.

Profiting by these favourable dispositions, Charney obtained from his munificence an allowance of pens, ink, and paper, wherewith to commemorate the sequel of his studies and observations on vegetable physiology; for the letter of the Governor of Turin did not go so far as to cancel the confiscation which had taken place of his former lucubrations. The two judiciary sbirri, after carrying off his cambric archives, and submitting them to the most careful examination, admitted their incompetency to discover a key to the cipher, and transmitted the whole to the minister of police in Paris, that more able decipherers might be employed to search out the root of the mystery.

But Charney had now to deplore a far more important privation. The commandant, resolved to visit upon Girardi, the only victim within his reach, the reprimand originally addressed to him by General Menon, had consigned the venerable Italian to a stronger part of the fortress, secure from all communication with the exterior, and the Count could not refrain from bitter self-reproaches, when he reflected upon the miserable isolation of the poor old man.

The greater portion of the day, his eyes remained mournfully fixed upon the grating in the wall, the little window of which was now closed up. In fancy he still beheld Girardi extending his arm through the bars, and trying to bestow upon him a friendly pressure of the hand; nay, he still seemed to see his precious memorial to the Emperor, fluttering against the wall and gradually drawn up from his own hands to those of Girardi,—thence to proceed to the hands of Teresa and the Empress. The very glance of pity and pardon cast down upon him by Girardi in his moment of anguish, seemed to shine ineffaceably on the spot; and often did he hear again the cry of exultation which burst from the window on the arrival of Picciola's reprieve. That very sentence of pardon is in fact the gift of Girardi and Girardi's daughter: and though solely serviceable to himself, has become the fatal origin of their separation and the sorrows of the parent and his child.

Even the countenance of Teresa was restored, by the efforts of his imagination, to the spot where alone it had been momentarily revealed to his eyes, at the close of the uneasy dream which he now believed to have foreshown the approaching perils of his plant. Inseparably united in his mind with the Picciola of his dreams, it was always under *her* form and features, that the living Teresa Girardi was revealed to him.

One day, as, with his eyes upraised towards the grating, the prisoner stood indulging in these and similar illusions, the dim and dusty window was flung open, and a female form appeared behind the grating. But the new-comer was a swarthy, savage-looking woman, with rapacious eyes, and an enormous goitre, in whom the Count soon recognised the wife of Ludovico.

From that moment, Charney never cast his eyes towards the window. The charm was broken.

CHAPTER II.

RELIEVED from all constraint, imbedded in new earth, and capaciously framed in the wide pavement, Picciola seemed to rise triumphantly from her tribulations. She had, however, survived her summer blossoms; with the exception of that single flower, the last to open and the last to fall.

Charney already foresaw important discoveries to be deduced from the seed, which was swelling and ripening in the calyx He promised himself the triumph of the *Dies Seminalis,* or Feast of the Sowers. For space was no longer wanting for his experiments: Picciola has more than enough room for her own expansion. She has every facility to become a mother, and shelter her uprising children under the shadow of her branches.

While waiting this important event, the Count becomes eager to ascertain the real name of the fair companion, to whom he is indebted for so many happy hours.

"Shall I never be able," thought Charney, "to bestow upon my foundling, my adopted child, the name she inherits from science, in common with her legitimate sisters of the plain or mountain?"

And at the first visit paid by the commandant to his charge, the Count admitted his desire to procure an elementary botanical work. Morand, unwilling either to refuse or to take upon himself the vast responsibility of compliance, thought proper to signify the demand in punctilious form to the governor of Piedmont. But from General Menon, the protégé of the Empress was now safe from a refusal; and a botanical dictionary soon arrived at the fortress, accompanied by all the folios treating of botany which could be obtained from the Royal Library of Turin.

"I have the honour," wrote General Menon, "to facilitate to the utmost the wishes of the Sieur Charney; for her Majesty the Empress-Queen, a proficient in botanical science, (as in many others,) will doubtless be glad to learn the name of a plant in whose welfare she has deigned to evince an interest."

When Ludovico made his appearance with the piles of books, under the enormous weight of which his back was breaking, Charney could not resist a smile.

"How!" cried he, "all this heavy artillery, to compel a poor helpless flower to give up her name?"

Nevertheless, it afforded him satisfaction to *look* once more upon a book. In turning over the leaves, his heart thrilled with pleasure, as in former days, when the attainment of knowledge was his chief delight in life. What months had now elapsed since printed characters were before his eyes! Already a plan of sage and sober study was concocting in his excited mind.

"If ever I am released from captivity," thought he, "I will certainly become a botanist. Instead of scholastic and pedantic controversies, which serve only to bewilder the human intellect, I will devote myself to a science where nature, ever varying, yet still the same, dispenses immutable laws to her disciples."

The books forwarded for the use of the Count de Charney. consisted of the *Species Plantarum*, of Linnæus; the *Institutiones rei Herbariæ* of Tournefort; the *Theatrum Botanicum* of Bauhin; and the *Phytographia, Dendrologia,* and *Agrostographia* of Plukenet, Aldrovandus, and Scheuchzer; besides half a hundred works of minor classicality, in the French, English, and Italian languages.

Though somewhat startled by so formidable an array of learning, the Count was not discouraged; and, by way of preparation for the worst, opened the thinnest volume of the collection, and began to examine the index in search of the most euphonous titles afforded by botanic nomenclature. He longed to appropriate to his purpose some of the softer saints of the floral calendar; such as Alcea, Alisma, Andryala, Bromelia, Celosia, Coronilla, Euphrasia, Helvelia, Passiflora, Primula, Santolina, or some other, equally soft to the lip, and harmonious to the ear.

And, now, for the first time, he began to tremble, lest his pretty favourite should inherit some quaint or harsh patronymic. A masculine or neuter termination would put to flight all his poetical vagaries concerning his gentle friend. What, for instance, would become of his ethereal Picciola, if her earthly prototype were to be saluted as *Rumex obtusifolius, Satyrium, Hoscyamus, Gossypium, Cynoglossum, Cucubalus, Cenchrus, Buxus;* or, worse still, and in more vulgar phrase, as Old Man, Dogtooth, Houndstongue, Cuckoo-flower, Devil-in-a-bush, Hen and Chickens, or Spiderwort! How should he support such a disenchantment of his nympholeptic imagination! No!—better not to risk the vexation of such an ordeal.

Yet, in spite of himself, he found it impossible to resist the temptation of opening every successive volume,—led on from page to page by the developement of the mighty mysteries of nature, but irritated by the love of system prevailing among the learned, by whom so charming a science has been rendered the harshest, most technical, and most perplexed, of all the branches of natural history.

For a whole week he devoted himself to the analysis of his flower, with a view to classification, but without success. In the chaos of so many strange words, varying from system to system,— bewildered by the vast and ponderous synonymy, which, like the net of Vulcan, overspreads the beauties of botany, overpowering them by its weight, he soon gave up the attempt; having consulted each author in succession, for a clew, wandering from classes to orders, from orders to tribes, from tribes to families, from families to species, from species to individuals; and losing all patience with the blind guides, ever at variance among themselves with respect to the purpose and denomination of the parts of organization in vegetable life.

At the close of his investigations, the poor little flower the last upon the tree, examined petal by petal, and to the very depth of her calyx, suddenly fell off one day into the hand of the operator, bearing with it Charney's hopes of inquiry into the progress of the seed, the reproduction of his favourite, the maternity of the lovely Picciola!

"She shall have no other title than PICCIOLA!" cried Charney. "Picciola, the flower of the captive. What do I want to know more of her name or nature? To what purpose this idle thirst after human knowledge?"

In a moment of petulance, Charney even threw down the vast heap of folios which had served to perplex him; when, from one of the volumes, came fluttering forth a slip of paper, on which had been recently inscribed, in the handwriting of a woman, the following verse, purporting to be a quotation from the Holy Scriptures:

"Hope, and bid thy neighbour hope: for, behold, I have not forsaken ye, and a day of consolation is at hand."

CHAPTER III.

CHARNEY perused and re-perused a hundred times a sentence which he could not but believe to have been especially addressed to himself. His correspondent was evidently a woman; but it grieved him to reflect that the only one to whom he was indebted for real acts of service, the only woman who had ever devoted herself to his cause, was still so imperfectly known to him, that he was ignorant of the very sound of her voice, and by no means sure of recognising her person, should she present herself before him.

But by what means had Teresa contrived to evade the vigilance of his Argus in the transmission of her letter?

Poor girl! Afraid to compromise her father by the mere mention of his name! Unhappy father!—to whom he is unable to afford consolation by the sight of the handwriting of his child!

Often, indeed, had Charney's nights been rendered sleepless by the idea of the solitary old man, to whom he had been the innocent cause of such irreparable injury, when one night, as he was lying awake, absorbed in these afflicting recollections, his ear was struck by an unaccustomed sound in the chamber above his own, which had remained uninhabited during the whole period of his confinement at Fenestrella.

Next morning, Ludovico entered his apartment, his countenance full of meaning, which he vainly attempted to compose to its usual vacuity of expression.

"What is the matter?" demanded the Coun. 'has any thing unusual occurred in the citadel?"

"Nothing particular, *Signor Conte;* nothing of any consequence, only we have had a sudden influx of prisoners; and the chambers of the northern and southern turrets being full, the commandant is under the necessity of placing another state prisoner in this part of the fortress, who must share with you the use of the court-yard. But this need be no hindrance to your pursuits. We receive at Fenestrella only gentlemen of high consideration,—that is, I mean we have no thieves or robbers among our prisoners. But stay, here *is* the new-comer, waiting to pay you his visit of inauguration."

Charney half rose at this announcement, scarcely knowing whether to grieve or rejoice at the intelligence; but, on turning to do the honours to his unexpected guest, what was his amazement to behold the door open for the admission of—Girardi!

After gazing upon each other for a moment in silence, as if still doubtful of the reality of their good fortune, the hands of the two prisoners were suddenly pressed together in mutual gratulations.

"Well and good," cried Ludovico, with a cordial smile; "no

need, I see, of a master of the ceremonies between you; the acquaintance has been quickly made:" and away he went, leaving them to the enjoyment of each other's society.

"To whom are we indebted, I wonder, for this happy meeting?" was Charney's first exclamation.

"To my daughter—doubtless to my daughter," replied Girardi. "Every consolation of my life reaches me through the hands of my Teresa."

"Do you know this handwriting?" inquired Charney, drawing from his casket the slip of paper he so dearly treasured.

"It is Teresa's!" cried Girardi; "it is the writing of my child! She has not neglected us; nor have her promises been tardy in their accomplishment. But how did this letter reach your hands?"

The Count related all the circumstances, then carelessly put forth his hand to receive back the slip of paper; but, perceiving that the poor old man silently detained it, perusing it word by word, letter by letter, and raising it a thousand times, with trembling hands, to his lips, he saw that the pledge was lost to him for ever; and experienced a regret at the loss, which appeared almost unaccountable.

After the first moments passed in conjectures, concerning Teresa and the spot where she was likely to have taken refuge, Girardi began to examine the lodgings of his new friend; and gravely proceeded to decipher the inscriptions on the wall. Two among them had been already modified; and the old man could readily discern, in this recantation, the influence exercised by Picciola over her votary. One of the maxims of Charney ran as follows:—"Mankind maintain, upon the surface of the earth, the position they will one day hold below it—side by side, without a single bond of union. Physically considered, the world is a mob, where millions meet and jostle together: morally speaking, it is a solitary wilderness."

To this withering sentence, the hand of Girardi added, "*Unless to him who has a friend.*" Then, turning to his young companion, the old man extended his arms towards him, and a mutual embrace sealed between them a compact of eternal friendship.

Next day, they dined together in the *camera* of the Count;—Charney seated upon the bed, and his venerable guest upon the chair,—the sculptured table between them being covered with double rations, viz: a fine trout from the lake of Avigliano, crayfish from the Cenise, a bottle of excellent Mondovi wine, and a piece of the celebrated Millesimo cheese, known over Italy under the name of *rubiola*. The feast was a noble one for a prison; but Girardi's purse was richly replenished, and the commandant willing to sanction every accommodation which Ludovico could afford to the two prisoners, within the letter of his instructions from head-quarters.

Never had Charney more thoroughly enjoyed the pleasures of the table. The happiest spirit of social intercourse was already established between them. If exercise, and the waters of the Eurotas, imparted a zest to the black broth of the Lacedæmonians, how much more the presence and conversation of a friend to the flavour of the choice viands of Piedmont!

Their hearts expanded with the sense of enjoyment. Without scruple, without preamble, but as if in fulfilment of the sacred engagements conveyed in their promises of friendship, Charney began to relate the presumptuous studies and idle vanities of his youth; while Girardi, by way of encouragement to this candour, did not hesitate to avow the early errors of his own.

CHAPTER IV.

Girardi was a native of Turin; in which city his progenitors had established a considerable manufactory of arms. From time immemorial, Piedmont has afforded a medium for the transmission of opinions and merchandise from Italy to France, and a medium for the transmission of merchandise and opinions from France to Italy; some portion of each, of course, being detained on the road. The breezes of France had breathed on Girardi's father, who was a philosopher, a reformer, a disciple of Voltaire: the breezes of Italy upon his mother, who was a zealot to the utmost extent of bigotry. The boy, loving and respecting both parents, and listening to both with equal confidence, participating in both their natures, became, of necessity, an amphibious moralist and politician. A republican, as well as a devotee, he was incessantly projecting the union of Liberty and Religion;—a holy alliance which he purposed to accomplish after a manner of his own. For Girardi was but twenty; and at that period, people were young at twenty years of age.

The enthusiastic youth was soon compelled to give pledges on both sides. The Piedmontese nobility retained certain nobiliary privileges,—such as an exclusive right to appear in a box at the theatre, or to dance at a public ball; and dancing was held to be an aristocratic exercise, in which the middle classes must content themselves with the part of spectators.

At the head of a band of young people of his own age, Giacomo Girardi chose, however, one day to infringe the national rule established by his betters; and at a public ball, headed a quadrille of untitled dancers, in the very face of the aristocratic portion of the assembly. The patrician dancers, indignant at the innovation, would fain have put a stop to the attempt; but vociferous cries of "*Amusement for all alike,—dancing for high and low*," were raised by the plebeians; and to this outbreak of sedition succeeded other cries of a liberal nature. In the tumult that ensued, twenty challenges were given and refused, not from cowardice, but pride; and the imprudent Giacomo, carried away by the impetuosity of his age and character, ended with inflicting a blow upon the proudest and most insolent of his adversaries.

The unpremeditated insult proved of serious moment. The influential family of San Marsano swore that it should not pass unpunished; the knights of St. Maurice, of the Annunciation, all the chivalry and nobility of the country (which an infringement of privilege is sure to render unanimous), affected to resent the offence, both individually and collectively. At his father's suggestion, the young man took refuge with one of his relations, vicar of a small village in the principality of Masserano, in the environs of Bielle, and, in consequence of his flight, Girardi was condemned, as contumacious, to five years' banishment from Turin.

The dignity to which the whole business was rashly elevated by all this notoriety, investing a boyish affray with the importance of a conspiracy, imparted considerable consequence to Giacomo Girardi in the eyes of his fellow-countrymen. Some saluted him as champion of the liberties of the people; others as one of those dangerous innovators who still dreamed of restoring the independence of Piedmont; but while, at the court of Turin, the insolent chastiser of nobility was denounced as a leading member of the democratic faction, the poor little partisan was quietly ministering to the performance of a village mass, after the fervent fulfilment of his own religious duties!

This stormy commencement of a life which had seemed predestined to peace and tranquillity, exercised a powerful influence over the fortunes of Giacomo Girardi. In his old age, he was fated to pay a severe penalty for the follies of his boyhood, for, upon his arrest on the groundless charge of having attempted the life of the First Consul, his accusers did not fail to recur to his early disorders, as an evidence of his dangerous tendency as a disturber of the public peace. But from the moment of quitting Turin, and during the whole period of his exile, Giacomo, indifferent to the love of equality instilled into him by his father, resigned himself to the influence of the religious principles derived from his mother. He even carried them to excess; and his relative, the worthy priest, whose faith was sincere, but whose capacity narrow and uncultivated, instead of checking the exalted fervour of the young enthusiast, excited it to the utmost, in the hope that the loveliness of Christian humility would impose a check upon the impetuosity of his character. But in the sequel, the worthy vicar repented the rashness of his calculations: for Giacomo would hear of nothing now but embracing the sacerdotal profession. The wild, hot-headed young man insisted on becoming a priest of the altar.

In the hope of arresting a measure which would deprive them of their only son, his father and mother got him recalled home; and by the utmost eloquence of parental tenderness, prevailed upon him to resign his projects, and acquiesce in their own. In a few months, Giacomo Girardi was married to a beautiful girl, selected for him by his family. But, to the great astonishment of his friends, the young fanatic not only persisted in regarding his lovely bride as an adopted sister, but exercised over her mind so strong an influence as to persuade her to retire into a convent, while *he* returned to his pious calling in the neighbourhood of Bielle.

At a short distance from his favourite village, rose the last branch of the Pennine Alps—a vast and towering chain of mountains; the highest peak of which, Monte Mucrone, overshadowed a gloomy little valley;—shaggy with overhanging rocks, obscured by mists, bordered by awful precipices, and appearing at a distance to imbody all the horrors with which Dante and Virgil have invested the entrance to the infernal regions. But on drawing nearer to the defile, the impending rocks were found to be clefted with verdure; the precipices to be relieved by gentle slopes, where flowering shrubs afforded a beautiful ladder of vegetation, interspersed with natural bowers and thickets; while the mists, varying in hue according to the reflections of the sun, after becoming white, pink, or violet, evaporated altogether under the influence of the noontide radiance. It was then that, deep in the lovely valley, a lake of about five hundred feet in length became apparent, alimented by crystal springs, and giving rise to the little river called the Oroppa, which at some distance farther encircled and formed into an island one of the verdant hillocks of the valley, on which the piety of the inhabitants has erected, at great cost, and consecrated to the Holy Virgin, one of the most remarkable churches in the country. If the legend is to be believed, St. Eusebius himself, on his return from a pilgrimage to the Holy Land, deposited there a wooden statue of the Virgin, carved by a hand no less holy than that of St. Luke the Evangelist, which he was desirous of securing from the profanations of the Arians.

In this sequestered vale, on the banks of this lonely lake, surrounded by the shrubby rocks and gentle precipices,—in this church, and at the foot of the miraculous statue, did Giacomo Girardi dream away five years of his young existence — rejecting the adoration of his lovely bride for that of the wooden lady of Oroppa!

Incapable of distinguishing between credulity and faith, unaware that superstition may degenerate into idolatry, that all extremes are unacceptable to GOD, he little suspected that it was not the Mary of Scripture—the mother of the Redeemer—to whom he dedicated his prayers; but a divinity of his own,—the tutelary genius of the place. Before the miraculous image, he passed his nights and days, in prayers and tears, praying for a higher spiritualization, and weeping over imaginary faults. His heart was that of a child,—his mind, that of a fanatic. In vain did the vicar, his worthy relative, labour to repress this unnatural fervour, and bring him back to reason. In vain, to distract his thoughts from one fixed and dangerous idea, did he suggest a pilgrimage to other spots of peculiar sanctity, dedicated to the worship of the Virgin. Giacomo would not hear of our Lady of Loretto, or the Saint Mary of Bologna or of Milan. He was infatuated by the pretended virtue of a material image, a piece of black and worm-eaten wood; and pronounced all homage to its celestial prototype.

The sentiments of the enthusiast, if they eventually lost in depth, gained only in extent. The Virgin of Oroppa was surrounded by a whole court of saints and saintesses;—and to each of these, the infatuated Giacomo assigned some peculiar duty of intercession. From one, he implored the dispersion of the clouds charged with hail-showers, which, from the heights of Monte Mucrone, sometimes rattled down upon his beloved valley. To another, he assigned the task of comforting his mother for his absence, and sustaining the spiritual weakness of his young wife. A third, he implored to watch over him in sleep,—a fourth, to defend him against the temptations of Satan. His devotion, by this means, degenerated into an impure polytheism, and Mount Oroppa into a new Olympus, where every divinity but the one Almighty GOD was honoured with a shrine.

Subjecting himself to the severest discipline, the most painful privations, he continued to macerate himself, to fast, to remain whole days without nourishment; and the exhaustion that ensued was qualified with the name of divine ecstacy! He saw visions, he heard revelations. After the delusions of the Quietists, he fancied that, by subjugating his physical nature, he could develope and render visible his soul. But, while resigning himself to this chimera, and holding imaginary discourse with his immaterial nature, Girardi's health gave way, and his reason became disordered.

One day, a voice seemed to address him from on high, commanding him to go and convert the heretic Waldenses, remnants of which persecuted sect still exist in the Valais. He accordingly set off, traversed the country adjoining the river Sesia, attained the summit of the Alps, near Monte Rosa, and there, suddenly arrested in his course by the snow of an early winter, found himself under the necessity of passing several months in a châlet.

This place of general refuge, designated, in the language of the country, *las strablas*, or the stables, consisted in a vast shed, five hundred feet square, open towards the south, but carefully closed in all other directions, by strong pine logs, filled in with moss and lichens, cemented into a mass by resinous gums. Here, in inclement weather, men, women, children, flocks, and herds, united together, as in a common habitation, under the control of the oldest member of the tribe. A large hearth, constantly supplied with fuel, sparkled in the centre of the dwelling; over which was suspended an enormous boiler, in which, alternately or together, the food of the community was prepared, — consisting of dried vegetables, pork, mutton, quarters of chamois, or cutlets of the flesh of the marmot; eaten afterwards at a general meal, with bread made of chestnut-meal, and a fermented liquor made from cranberries and whortleberries.

Occupations were not wanting in the châlet. The children and flocks were to be attended to; the winter cheeses to be made; the spinning, which was incessantly at work; and instruments of husbandry, in progress of manufacture, to force into cultivation, during the short summer season, the shallow soil of the adjacent rocks. Garments of sheep-skin were also manufactured; baskets of the bark of trees; and a variety of elegant trifles, carved in sycamore, or larchwood, for sale in the nearest towns. The population of the châlet, cheerful and laborious, suffered not an hour to pass unimproved; and songs and laughter intermingled with the strokes of the axe, and busy murmur of the wheel. Labour scarcely appeared a task; and study and prayer were accounted the duty and recreation of the day. Harmonious and well-practised voices united in chorus for the daily execution of pious canticles: the elder shepherds instructed the young in reading and arithmetic; —nay, even in music, and a smattering of Latin; for the civilization of the Higher Alps, like its vegetation, seems to be preserved under the snow; and it is no uncommon thing to see, at the return of spring, school-masters and minstrels descend from the châlets, to diffuse knowledge and hilarity among the agricultural villages of the plain.

The worthy hosts of Giacomo proved to be Waldenses. The opportunity was an auspicious one for the young apostle; but, scarcely had he let fall a word of the purport of his mission, when the octogenarian chief of the community, high in the renown, so cured, among these humble peasants, by a life of industry and virtue, cut short his expectations.

"Our fathers," said he to the young man, "endured exile, persecutions, death,—rather than subscribe to the image-worship practised among your people. Hope not, therefore, that your feeble powers will effect what centuries of persecution failed to accomplish. Stranger! you have found shelter under our roof, and therein, for your own safety, must abide. Pray, therefore, to God, according to the dictation of your own conscience, as we do according to ours; but be advised by the experience of a gray-beard, and take part in the labours proceeding around you; or, in this solitude, remote from the rumours and excitements of social life, want of occupation will destroy you. Be our companion, our brother, so long as the winter snows weigh upon your existence and our own; and, at the return of spring, leave us, unquestioned, as you came; without so much as bestowing your benediction on our hearth:—nay, without even turning back upon your path, to salute, by a farewell gesture, those by whose fire you have been warmed, and at whose frugal board, nourished. For, having shared their industry, you will owe them nothing. The fruit of your own labour will have maintained you; and, should any debt be still owing, the God of mercy will repay us a thousand-fold for our hospitality to the son of the stranger."

Forced to submit to a proposition so reasonable, Giacomo remained five months an inmate of the châlet, and an eye-witness of the virtuous career of its inhabitants. Night and morning, he heard their prayers and thanksgivings offered up to the throne of grace,—to the throne of the one omnipresent GOD; and his mind, no longer excited by the objects which had wrought its exaltation, became gradually composed to a reasonable frame. When the prison of ice, constructed for him by nature, ceased to hold him captive, and the sun, shining out with the return of spring, developed before his eyes all the beauty and majesty of the mountain-scenery by which he was surrounded, the idea of the Almighty Lord of the universe seemed to manifest itself powerfully to his mind, and resume its fitting influence on his heart.

The geniality of the weather, reviving all nature around him, with her swarming myriads of birds and bees hovering over the new-born flowers, starting anew to life from beneath their winter mantle of snow, awoke in his bosom correspondent transports of love and joy. It were vain to dilate on the expansion of human feeling which gradually enlarged his perceptions. The good old chief had begun to entertain an affection for him; and, though unlearned in pedantic lore, had stored up, in the course of his long existence, an infinity of facts and observations, which, joined to those inherited from the lessons of his fathers, inspired him with knowledge of the Creator through the wisdom of his works. In a word, the presumptuous youth, who had entered that humble asylum for the purpose of converting its people to his opinions, eventually quitted it, *himself* converted to their own!—nay, the industrious habits he had acquired, and the examples of domestic happiness he had witnessed, had brought him to a due sense of his error in neglecting the happiness and duties with which Providence had endowed his existence.

Giacomo's first visit after quitting Monte Rosa, was to the convent in which his wife was immured. A whole romance might be developed in the history of his wooing, and the difficulties with which his courtship was beset. Suffice it, that after many months devoted to the obliteration of the lessons he had himself inculcated, Girardi, aided by the influence of his parents, succeeded in removing his wife from the cloistral seclusion to which he had devoted her; and became, in the sequel, the happiest of husbands and of fathers.

The errors of his youth were now redeemed by years of wisdom and of virtue. Established in his native city of Turin, in the enjoyment of a handsome fortune, the thriving speculations in which he was engaged might have rendered it colossal, but for the systematic benevolence which rendered the opulence of Girardi a second providence to the poor. To do good was the *occupation* of his life; his favourite recreation was the study of animated nature. Girardi became a proficient in natural history; and as GOD is greatest in the least of his works, entomology chiefly engaged his attention. It was this interest in the organization and habits of insects, which had obtained for him from Ludovico, in the earlier stages of his imprisonment, the appellation of "The Fly-catcher."

CHAPTER V.

THE two prisoners had no longer any secrets from each other! After glancing rapidly over the history of their several lives, they returned to the various incidents of each, and the emotions to which they had given rise. They sometimes spoke of Teresa; but at the very mention of her name, a vivid blush overspread the face of Charney, and the old man himself grew grave and sad. Any allusion to the absent angel was sure to be followed by an interval of mournful silence.

Their discourse usually turned upon the discussion of some

point of morality; or comments upon the eccentricities of human nature. Girardi's philosophy, mild and benevolent, invested the happiness of man in the love of his fellow-creatures; nor could Charney, though half converted to his opinions, understand by what means this spirit of tenderness and indulgence could survive the injuries which the philosopher had endured from mankind.

"Surely," said he, "you must have bestowed your malediction on those who, after basely calumniating you, tore you from the bosom of domestic happiness,—from the arms of——your daughter?"

"The offence of a few," replied Girardi, "was not to subvert my principles of action towards the whole. Even those few, blinded by political fanaticism, fancied they were fulfilling a duty. Trust me, my young friend, it is indispensable to survey even the injuries we receive through a medium of pardon and pity. Which of us has not required forgiveness for faults? Which of us has not, in his turn, mistaken error for the truth? St. John bequeathed to us the blessed axiom that GOD IS LOVE! True and beautiful proposition!—since by love alone the soul re-elevates itself to its celestial source, and finds courage for the endurance of misfortune! Had I entered into captivity with a particle of hatred in my soul against my fellow-creatures, I should have expired in my imbittered loneliness. But Heaven be praised, I have never been the prey of a single painful reflection. The recollection of my good and faithful friends, whose hearts I knew were suffering with every suffering of my own, served to stimulate my affection towards mankind; and the only unlucky moment of my captivity was that in which I was debarred the sight of a fellow-creature."

"How!" cried Charney, "were you ever subjected to such a deprivation?"

"At my first arrest," resumed Girardi, "I was transported to a dungeon in the citadel of Turin; so framed as to render communication impossible even with my gaoler. My food was conveyed to me by a turning box inserted in the wall; and during a whole month not the slightest sound interrupted the stillness of my solitude. It needs to have undergone all I then experienced, fully to comprehend the fallacy of that savage philosophy which denied society to be the natural condition of the human species. The wretch condemned to isolation from his kind is a wretch indeed! To hear no human voice,—to meet no human eye,—to be denied the pressure of a human hand,—to find only cold and inanimate objects on which to rest one's brow,—one's breast,—one's heart; —is a privation to which the strongest might fall a victim! The month I thus endured weighed like years upon my nature; and when, every second day, I discerned the footsteps of my gaoler in the corridor, coming to renew my provisions, the mere sound caused my heart to leap within me. While the box was turning round, I used to strain my eyes in hopes to catch, at the crevice, the slightest glimpse of his face, his hand, his very dress; and my disappointment drove me to despair. Could I have discerned a human face, even bearing the characters of cruelty or wickedness, I should have thought it full of beauty; and had the man extended his arms towards me in kindness, have blessed him for the concession! But the sight of a human face was denied me till the day of my translation to Fenestrella; and my only resource consisted in feeding the reptiles which shared my captivity, and in meditating upon my absent child!"

Charney started at the allusion: but his venerable companion was himself too much distressed to notice the emotion of his young friend.

"At length," said he, after a long pause, which served to restore him to his usual serenity, " a favourable change befel me even in my dungeon. I discovered, by means of a straggling ray of light, a crevice produced by the insertion of an iron cross by way of support into the walls of my dungeon: which, though it enabled me to obtain only an oblique glimpse of the opposite wall, became a source of exquisite enjoyment. My cell happened to be situated under the keep of the citadel; and one blessed day, I noticed for the first time the shadow of a man distinctly reflected upon the wall. A sentinel had doubtless been posted on the platform over my head; for the shadow went and came, and I could distinguish the form of the man's uniform, the epaulet, the knapsack, the point of his bayonet,—the very vacillation of his feather!

"Till evening extinguished my resource, I remained at my post; and how shall I describe the thrill of joy with which I acknowledged so unexpected a consolation! I was no longer alone; —I had once more a living companion!—Next day and the days succeeding, the shadow of another soldier appeared; the sentinels were ever changing, but my enjoyment was the same. It was always a man,—always a fellow-creature I knew to be near me;— a living, breathing fellow-creature,—whose movements I could watch, and whose dispositions conjecture. When the moment came for relieving guard, I welcomed the new-comer, and bade good-by to his predecessor. I knew the corporal by sight; I could recognise the different profiles of the men; nay, (dare I avow such a weakness!) some among them were objects of my predilection. The attitude of their persons, or comparative vivacity of their movements, became so many indications of character, from which their age and sentiments might be inferred. One paced gaily along, turning lightly on his heel, balancing his musket in sport, or waving his head in cadence to the air he was whistling; *he* was doubtless young and gay, cheered by visions of happiness and love. Another paced along, with his brow inclining, pausing often, and leaning with his arms crossed upon his musket, meditating mournfully, perhaps, upon his distant village, his absent mother, his childhood's friends. He passed his hand rapidly over his eyes—perhaps to dash away the tears gathered by these tender retrospections!

"For many of these shadows I felt a lively interest, an inexplicable compassion; and the balm thus called into existence within my bosom shed its soothing influence over my fate. Trust me, my good young friend, the truest happiness is that we derive from our sympathy with our fellow-creatures."

"Why did I not become earlier acquainted with you, excellent man?" cried Charney, deeply affected. "How different, then, had been the tenor of my life! But what right have I to complain? Have I not found in this desolate spot all that was denied me amid the splendour of the world?—a devoted heart—a noble soul — an anchor of strength! — virtue and truth — Girardi and Picciola?"

For among all these effusions of the heart, Picciola was not forgotten. The two friends had constructed a more capacious seat beside her; where, side by side, and facing the lovely plant, they passed hour after hour together, all three in earnest conversation. Charney had given to this new seat the name of "The Bench of Conference."

There did the simple-minded Girardi aspire for once to eloquence: for without eloquence in the expositor, no conviction. Nor were the eloquence or conviction wanting.

The bench had become the rostrum of a professor; a professor, though less learned than his scholar, infinitely wiser and more enlightened. The professor is Giacomo Girardi, the pupil the Count de Charney, and the book in process of exposition — Picciola!

CHAPTER VI.

As autumn approached, Charney could not forbear expressing to his friend, as they sat together on the Bench of Conference, his regret at losing all hopes of Picciola's second flowering, and his lamentations over her last blossom.

Girardi immediately attempted to supply the loss by a dissertation on the fructification of plants, and the evidence thereby afforded of the intervention of an all-wise Providence.

Girardi first alluded to the winged form of the seeds of certain plants, whose foliage, large and complicated, would oppose their dispersion, but for the feathery tuft attached to each, which causes them to float in the atmosphere; and described the elastic pods in which others are enclosed, which, opening by a sudden spring, at the moment of maturity, discharge the seed to a distance. "These wings, these springs," observed the old man, "are hands and feet bestowed upon them by the Almighty, that they may reach their destined place, and germinate in the sunshine. What human eye, for instance," said he, "is able to follow, in their aerial flight, the membranous seeds of the elm, the maple, the pine, the ash— circling in the atmosphere amid volumes of other seeds, rising by their own buoyancy, and apparently flying in search of the birds, of which they are to form the nourishment?"

The old man next proceeded to explain the phenomena of aquatic plants; how the seeds of those destined for the adornment of brooks, or the banks of lakes or ponds, are endowed with a form enabling them to float upon the water, so as to deposit themselves in various parts of the beach, or cross from one bank to another; while such as are intended to take root in the bed of the river fall at once by their own weight to the bottom, and give birth to reeds and rushes, or those beautiful water-lilies, whose roots are in the mud beneath, while their large green shining leaves, and snow-white blossoms, float in pride and glory upon the bosom of the waters. The vallisneria was not forgotten; the male and female plants of which being disunited, the former uncoils her long spiral peduncle, to raise her flower above the surface of the stream, while the male, unpossessed of a similar faculty, breaks its fragile flower-stalk, and rises spontaneously to the surface, to accomplish the act of fecundation.

"How is it," cried Charney, "that men remain insensible to the existence of these wondrous prodigies of nature?"

And the old man rejoiced at the exclamation, as a proof that his lessons were not shed upon a barren and ungrateful soil.

"Tell me," demanded the Count, "has the insect creation, to which your studies have been peculiarly addressed, furnished you with facts as curious as those for which I am indebted to my Picciola?"

"*So* curious," replied Girardi, "that you will not fully appreciate even the marvels of Picciola till you have become acquainted with the hosts of animated beings which hover over her verdant branches. You will then learn to admire the secret laws which connect the plant with the insect, the insect with the plant; and perceive that 'order is Heaven's first law,' and that one vast intelligence influences the whole creation."

Girardi was proceeding to enlarge upon the harmony of the

universe, when, pausing suddenly, he pointed out to his companion a brilliant and beautiful butterfly, poised on one of the twigs of his plant, with a peculiar quivering of the wings. "See!" cried he, "Picciola hastens to expound my theory! An engagement has just been contracted between her and yonder insect, which is now consigning its posterity to her guardianship."

And when the butterfly flew away, Charney verified the assertion by examining a little group of eggs, attached by a viscous substance to the bark.

"Do you imagine," inquired Girardi, "that it is by chance the butterfly has proceeded hither, to intrust to Picciola this precious deposit? On the contrary, Nature has assigned to every plant analogies with certain insects. Every plant has its insect to lodge, its insect to feed. Admire the long chain of connexion between them! This butterfly, when a caterpillar, was nourished on the substance of a plant of the same species as Picciola; and after undergoing its appointed transformations, and become a butterfly, it fluttered faithless from flower to flower, sipping the sweets of a thousand different nectaries. But no sooner did the moment of maturity arrive for a creature that never beheld its mother, and will never behold its children, (for its task fulfilled, it is now about to die,) than, by an instinct surer than the best lessons of experience, it flew hither to deposit its progeny on a plant similar to that by which, under a different form and in a different season, it was fed and protected. Instinctively conscious that little caterpillars will emerge from its eggs, it forgets, for their sake, the habits it has acquired as a butterfly!

"Who taught her all this? Who endowed her with memory, powers of reasoning, and recognising the peculiarities of a vegetable, whose present foliage bears no resemblance to that which it bore during the spring? The most experienced botanist is often mistaken—the insect, never!"

Charney involuntarily testified his surprise.

"You have still more to learn," interrupted Girardi. "Examine the branch selected by the insect. It is one of the largest and strongest on the tree; not one of the new shoots, likely to be decayed by frost during the winter, or broken by the wind. All this has been foreseen by the insect. Whence did it derive such prescience?"

"Do you not in some degree deceive yourself, my dear friend?" demanded Charney, unwilling to avow how much he was confounded by these discoveries.

"Peace, sceptic, peace!" replied the old man, with an accusing smile. "You will admit, at least, that seeing is believing! Picciola has now *her* part to play. The foresight of the insect is not greater than that with which Nature endows the plant towards the legacy bequeathed by the butterfly; at the return of spring we will verify the prodigy together. The moment the plant puts forth its leaves, the tiny eggs will break, and emit the larvæ they contain: a law of harmony regulates the vegetation of the plant in common with the vitality of the insect. Were the larvæ to appear first, there would be no food for them; were the leaves to precede them, they would have acquired too firm a consistency for their feeble powers. But Nature, provident over all, causes both plant and insect to develope themselves at the same moment, to grow together, and together attain their maturity; so that the wings and flowers of each are simultaneous in their display of beauty."

"Another lesson derived from my gentle Picciola!" murmured the astonished Charney; and conviction entered into his soul!

Thus passed the days of the captives, in mutual solace and instruction; and when, every evening, the hour arrived for retreating singly into the camera of each, to wait the hour of rest, the same object unconsciously occupied their meditations; for Charney thought of Teresa, and Girardi of his daughter, exhausting their minds in conjecture as to her present destiny.

The young girl herself, meanwhile, was not inactive on their behalf. Her first impulse had been to follow the Emperor to Milan; where Teresa soon discovered that it is as difficult to penetrate through the antechamber of royalty as through the ranks of an army. The friends of Girardi, however, roused by her efforts, renewed their applications, and having undertaken to procure, at no remote period, the liberation of the captive, his daughter, somewhat reassured, returned to Turin, where an asylum was offered her in the house of a near relation.

The husband of this relative happened to be the librarian of the city; and to him did Menon address himself, to select the botanical works destined for the use of the prisoner of Fenestrella. It was no difficult matter for Teresa to infer from the nature of the study to whom these books were destined; and she accordingly managed to slip into one of the volumes the mysterious despatch, which, even if discovered by the commandant, was not of a nature to compromise either her relation or the *protégé* in whose behalf she had already ventured so largely. She was still ignorant that her father and Charney no longer resided in each other's neighbourhood; and when the news of their separation was brought back by the messenger employed to convey the books to Fenestrella, it became her first object to accomplish the reunion of the two captives.

After addressing letter after letter on the subject, to the governor of Piedmont, she continued to interest in her behalf some of the chief inhabitants of Turin, and, through them, the wife of Menon, till the general, having strong motives for desiring to conciliate his influential petitioners, ended by granting the prayer of Teresa Girardi. And when, under the auspices of Madame Menon, she came to offer her grateful thanks to the general, the veteran, touched by the devotedness of her filial tenderness, laying aside for a moment the harshness of his nature, took the young girl kindly by the arm, as he addressed her.

"You must come and visit my wife from time to time," said he. "In about a month's time she may have good news to tell you."

And Teresa, nothing doubting that the good news would consist in an order for her readmission into the fortress of Fenestrella, to pass a portion of every day with her father, threw herself at the feet of the general with a countenance bright with joy, loading him with grateful acknowledgments.

While all this was proceeding undreamed of by the two captives, Charney and Girardi sat enjoying on their bench a glorious October sunshine, restoring, or rather forestalling around them, the warmth and promise of spring. Both were pensive and silent, leaning severally on the opposite arms which closed in the rustic seat. They might have passed for estranged or indifferent to each other, but for the wistful looks cast from time to time by Charney upon his companion, who was absorbed in a profound reverie. It was not often that the countenance of Girardi was overshadowed by sadness—no wonder, therefore, that the Count should mistake the motives of his depression.

"Yes!" cried he, replying, as he fancied, to the looks of his friend; "captivity is, indeed, a purgatory! To be imprisoned for an imaginary offence,—to live apart from all we love."

But ere he could proceed, Girardi, raising his head, gazed with surprise upon the Count. "True, my dear friend!" he replied. "separation is one of the severest trials of human fortitude!"

"*I* your friend!" interrupted Charney, with bitterness. "Have you the charity to bestow such a name upon *me*—upon me, who am the cause of your being parted from her? for it is of your daughter you are thinking! Deny it not! Teresa is the object of these mournful meditations; and, at such a moment, how odious must I be in your sight!"

"Believe me, you are mistaken in your conjectures," mildly interrupted the venerable man. "Never was the image of my daughter invested with such consolatory associations as to-day. For Teresa has written to me:—I have received a letter from my child."

"Written to you,—you have a letter from her,—they have suffered it to reach your hands!" cried Charney, insensibly drawing nearer to his companion. Then checking his exultation, he added, " But you have, doubtless, learned some afflicting tidings?"

" Far from it, I assure you."

" Wherefore, then, this depression?"

" Alas! my dear friend, such is the frailty of human nature; such is the mingled yarn of human destiny! A regret is sure to embitter our sweetest hopes. The happiness of this life casts its shadow before, and it is by the shadow that our attention is first attracted. You spoke of separation from those we love. Here is my letter!—read it, and learn what considerations depress my spirits while seated by your side."

Charney took the letter, and for some moments held it unopened in his hand:—his eyes fixed on the countenance of Girardi, he seemed desirous of reading *there* the intelligence it contained. On examining the address he recognised with emotion the handwriting of his precious billet; and at length unfolding the paper, attempted to read aloud the contents. But his voice faltered,—the words expired upon his lips; and stopping short, he concluded the letter almost inaudibly to himself.

" Dearest father," wrote Teresa, " bestow a thousand kisses upon the paper you hold in your hands; for a thousand and a thousand have I impressed upon it, as harvest for your venerated lips!

" What joy for us both, this renewal of correspondence! It is to General Menon we are indebted for the concession;—he it is who has put an end to a silence which, even more than distance, seemed to keep us asunder. Blessings be upon him! *Now*, dear father, our thoughts, at least, may fly towards each other;—*I* shall communicate my hopes to sustain your courage; *you*, your griefs, in weeping over which I shall fancy I am weeping in your presence! But if a greater happiness, dearest father, were in reserve for us! For a moment, I beseech you, lay aside my letter, and summon your strength to hear the sudden joy I am about to excite in your bosom. Father! If I were once more permitted to be with you!—to approach you,—to listen to your instruction,—to surround you with my attentions! Throughout the two years in which we enjoyed this alleviation of our affliction, captivity seemed to sit lightly on your spirits; and I entertain the hope,—yes, the earnest, earnest hope, that the favour will be again vouchsafed me;—that I shall be once more permitted to enter your prison!"

" Teresa about to visit you!—here in the fortress!" cried Charney, wild with joy.

" Read on!"—replied the old man, in a melancholy tone,—" read on!"

" I shall be once more permitted to enter your prison," resumed Charney, repeating the last sentence. " Are you not happy in such a prospect? Are you not overjoyed?" continued Teresa. "Pause a moment, to consider the good tidings I have thus announced! Do not hurry on towards the conclusion of my letter. Violent emotions are sometimes dangerous. Have I not already said enough? Were an angel to descend from heaven, charged with the accomplishment of our wishes, you would not presume to require more; but I, your child, might venture, ere he reascended to his native skies, *I* might be tempted to implore your liberation from captivity. At *your* age, father, it is a cruel thing to be denied the sight of your native country. The banks of our beloved Doria are so beautiful; and in our gardens on the Collina, the trees planted by my poor mother and brother have acquired surprising growth during your absence. There, more than on any other spot, survives the precious memory of those we have lost.

"Then, father, there are your friends;—the friends who have supported, by their generous efforts, my applications to government. I am sure you regret your absence from them; I am sure you would delight in seeing them again. Oh! father, father! the pen seems to burn in my hand! My secret is about to escape me! It has, probably, already escaped me! You have, doubtless, summoned all your courage to learn definitively that, in a few days, I am about to rejoin you, *not* to lend my aid in softening your captivity, but to announce its termination; *not* to be with you at stated hours, and within the walls of a prison; but to carry you away with me in triumph from Fenestrella;—free, proud,—ay, proud!—for you have now a right to resume your pride. Your faithful friends, Cotenna and Delarue, did not rest till they obtained, *not* your pardon, but your justification. Yes, your innocence is fully recognised by the imperial government.

"Farewell, dearest and best of fathers. How I love you! how happy do I feel at this moment! and how much happier shall I be when again folded in your arms! Your own

"TERESA."

The letter did not contain a single word in reference to Charney. That word—that hoped-for word—how eagerly did he seek for it in every page and line!—how eagerly, and how vainly. Yet, notwithstanding his disappointment, it was a cry of joy that burst from the lips of the Count, when he concluded the letter.

"You will soon be free!" cried he; "soon able to rest under the shadow of green trees, and behold the rising of the sun!"

"Yes!" replied the old man. "But I am also about to *leave you!* Such is the shadow which precedes my happiness to-day, to prevent my joy from falling into excess."

"Think not of *me*, I beseech you!" cried Charney; proving, by his generous transports, and forgetfulness of self, how truly he deserved the friendship of which he was the object. "At last, you will be restored to her arms! At last, she will cease to suffer from the consequence of my rashness! *You* will be happy, and I no longer oppressed by the heaviness of remorse. During the last few hours that remain for us to be together, we may at least talk of her unreservedly."

And, as he uttered these last incoherent words, the Count de Charney threw himself into the arms of his venerable friend.

CHAPTER VII.

THE knowledge of their approaching separation seemed only to augment the tender affection existing between the two friends. Seldom an hour apart, both seemed eager to continue till the last moment their conferences on the bench of the little court.

There was a solemn subject, to which Girardi often endeavoured to lead the way; but Charney invariably evaded the discussion. The old man was, however, too deeply interested in sounding the opinions of the Count to be easily discouraged; and one day an occasion unexpectedly presented itself for the accomplishment of his wishes.

"How unaccountable the chance," cried Charney, after a short silence, "which united us in this place; naturally divided as we are by difference of birth-place, of languages, of faith, of prejudices! Yet, in spite of all these obstacles, we have met at Fenestrella, to unite in the same religious principles, the same adoration of the one supreme Being."

"On that point, give me leave to differ with you," said Girardi, with a smile. "To lose sight of, is not to deny. Our views have never been the same."

"Certainly not. But which of the two, the bigot or the sceptic, was most mistaken?—which the most deserving pity?"

"Yourself!" replied the old man, without hesitation,— "yes, my dear young friend, yourself! All extremes are dangerous; but in superstition, there is faith, passion, vitality; and in scepticism, universal night,—universal death. Superstition is the pure stream diverted from its natural channel, which inundates, submerges, and displaces the vegetable soil; but conveys it elsewhere, and repairs, farther on its course, the injuries it has produced; while scepticism is drought, dearth, sterility; burning and scorching up, transmuting earth to sand, and rendering the mighty Palmyra a ruin of the desert. Not content with placing an eternal bar betwixt us and the Creator, incredulity relaxes the bonds of society, and destroys the ties of kindred and affection. In depriving man of his importance as a being eternally responsible, it creates around him isolation and contempt. He is alone in the world,—alone with his pride; or, as I said before, alone as a ruin in the desert."

"Alone with his *pride!*" murmured Charney, reclining his elbow on the arm of the bench, and his face upon his hand. "Pride!—of what!—of knowledge?—of science? Oh! why should man labour to destroy the elements of his happiness, by seeking to analyze them, or to sound their depths? Even if indebted for his joys to a deception, why seek to raise the mask, and accelerate the disenchantment of his future life? Is truth so dear to him? Does knowledge suffice the desires of his ambition? Madman!—such was my own delusion. 'I am but a worm,' said I to myself, 'a worm destined to annihilation:' then, raising myself in the dust where I was crawling, I felt proud of the discovery,—vain of my helpless nakedness. I believed neither in virtue nor happiness; but, at the thought of annihilation, I stopped proudly short, and accorded my unlimited faith. My degradation appeared a triumph to me,—for it was assured by a discovery of my own. Was I not justified in my estimation of a theory, for which I had given in exchange no less than my regal mantle,—the countless treasure of my immortality?"

The old man extended his hand encouragingly towards his companion.

"Be judged by your own image of the worm," said Girardi. "The worm, after crawling its season on the earth, fed with bitter leaves, condemned to the slime of the marsh, or the dust of the road, constructs his own chrysalis, a temporary coffin; from which to emerge, transformed, purified,—to flutter from flower to flower, and feed upon their precious perfumes. On two radiant wings, the new creature takes its flight towards the skies, even as man, the image of his Creator, rises to the bosom of his God."

Charney replied by a negative movement of the head.

"Your disease was more deeply rooted than my own," observed Girardi, with a mournful smile, "for your convalescence, I see, will be more tedious. Have you already forgot the lessons of Picciola?"

"Not one of them!" replied Charney, in a tone of deep emotion. "I believe in GOD. I believe in a first cause. I believe in an omniscient Power, the eternal Controller of the universe. But your comparison of the worm supposes the immortality of the soul; and by what is it demonstrated to my reason?"

"By the instincts of the human soul, which irresistibly impel us to look forward with hope and joy. Our life is a life of expecation. From infancy to old age, hope is the dominating pole of our destinies. In what savage nation of the earth has not the doctrine of a future state been found existent? And why should not the hope thus conceded be accomplished? Is the power of God more infinite than the mind of his creatures? I do not invoke the authority of revelation and the Holy Scriptures. All convincing to myself: for *you* they possess no authority. The breeze which impels the ship, is powerless to move the rock: for the rock has no expanding sails to receive its impulse, and its feet are buried in the ponderous immobility of earth. Shall we believe in the eternity of matter, and not in that of the intelligence which serves to regulate our opinions concerning matter? Or are we to suppose that love, virtue, genius, result from the affinity of certain terrestrial molecules? Can that which is devoid of thought enable us to think? Can brute matter be the basis of human intelligence, when human intelligence is able to direct and govern matter? Why then do not stocks and stones think and feel as we do?"

"Locke, the great English metaphysician, was inclined to suppose that matter might be endowed with ideas," observed Charney "There was contradiction, indeed, in his theory, since he rejected the doctrine of innate ideas, and seemed to admit the possibility of intuitive knowledge." Then interrupting himself with a laugh, the Count exclaimed, "Have a care, my kind instructor! I see you would fain involve me once more in the quicksand of doubt, or plunge me into the bottomless pit of metaphysics!"

"I have no knowledge of metaphysics," said Girardi, gravely.

"And I but little," observed Charney; "not, however, for want of devoting my time to the study. But let us drop a subject unprofitable, and, perhaps, injurious. You believe,—rejoice in your belief! Your faith is dear to you; and if, perchance, I should shake its foundations"—

"I defy you to the contest!" cried Girardi.

"What have you to gain by the result?"

"Your conversion; nothing less, my dear young friend, than your conversion. Just now you quoted Locke. Of that eminent philosopher I know but a single trait;—that through life, and even on his death-bed, he asserted the true happiness of mankind to consist in purity of conscience, and hope in eternal life."

"I perfectly comprehend the *consolation* to be derived from such a creed; but my better reason forbids me to accept it. I entreat you, let us drop the subject," said the Count de Charney.

And a constrained silence ensued.

Soon afterwards, something which had been circling overhead, suddenly alighted on the foliage of the plant; a greenish insect, of which the narrow corslet was undulated with whitish stripes.

"Sir!" cried Charney, "behold in good time a new text enabling you to enlarge upon the mysteries of creation."

Girardi took the insect with due precaution: examined it carefully; paused for reflection; and suddenly an expression of triumph developed itself in his countenance. An irresistible argument seemed to have fallen from heaven in his hands. Commencing in his usual professional tone, he gradually assumed a more sublime expression, as the secret object of his lesson penetrated through his language.

"Mere fly-catcher as I am," he began with an arch smile, "I must restrict myself to my humble attributions, and not presume to affect the pedantry of the scholar."

"The most enlightened mind," said Charney, "the mind which has profited most largely by the acquirement of knowledge, is that which soonest discovers the limitation of its own powers, after vainly attempting to penetrate into the hidden mysteries of things. Genius itself breaks its wings against such obstacles, without having extracted from the wall of flints, by which it is obstructed, one spark of the light of truth."

"We ignoramuses," observed Girardi, "arrive sooner at our object, by taking the most direct road. If we do but open our eyes, GOD deigns to reveal himself in the august sublimity of his works."

"On that point we are agreed," interrupted Charney.

"Proceed we then in our course. An herb of the field sufficed to prove to you the existence of a Providence; a butterfly, the law of universal harmony: the insect before us, of which the organization is of a still higher order, may lead us still farther towards conviction."

Charney, at the instance of his friend, proceeded to examine the little stranger with curious attention.

"Behold this insignificant creature," resumed Girardi. "All that human genius could effect, would not add one tittle to an organization, perfectly adapted to its wants and necessities. It has wings to transport it from one place to another; elytra to incase and secure them from the contact of any hard substance. Its breast is defended by a cuirass, its eyes by a curious network that defies the prick of a thorn or the sting of an enemy. It possesses antennæ to interrogate the obstacles that present themselves, —feet to attain its prey,—iron mandibles to assist in devouring it, in digging the earth for a refuge, or a depository for its food or eggs. If a dangerous adversary should approach, it has in reserve an acrid and corrosive fluid, by discharging which it defies its enemies. Instinct teaches it to find its food, to provide its lodg ing, and exercise its powers of offence and defence. Nor is this a solitary instance. Other insects are endowed with similar delicacy of organization;—the imagination recoils with wonder from the multiplicity and variety of provisions invented by nature for the security of the apparently feeble insect tribe. We have still to consider this fragile creature as demonstrating the line of demarcation between mankind and the brute creation.

"Man is sent naked into the world,—feeble, helpless,—unendowed with the wings of a bird, the swiftness of the stag, the tortuous speed of the serpent; without means of defence against the claws or darts of an enemy, nay, against even the inclemency of the weather. He has no shell, no fleece, no covering of fur, nor even a den or burrow for his hiding-place. Yet by force of his natural powers, he has driven the lion from his cave,—despoiled the bear of his shaggy coat for a vestment, and the bull of his horn to form a drinking-cup. He has dug into the entrails of the earth, to bring forth elements of future strength; the very eagle, in traversing the skies, finds itself struck down in the midst of its career to adorn his cap with a trophy of distinction.

"Which of all the animal creation could have supported itself in the midst of such difficulties and such privations? Let us for a moment suppose the disunion of power and action,—of God and nature. Nature has done wonders for the insect before us; for man, apparently nothing. Because man, an emanation from God himself, and formed after his image, was created feeble and helpless as regards the organization of matter, in order to demonstrate the divine influence of that ethereal spark, which endows him with all the elements of future greatness."

"Explain to me, at least," interrupted Charney, "the peculiar value of this precious gift, bestowed, you say, exclusively upon the human species;—superior in many points to the animal creation, surely we are inferior in the majority. This very insect, whose wondrous powers you have expounded, inspires me with a sense of inferiority and profound humiliation."

"From time immemorial," replied Girardi, "animals have displayed no progress in their powers of operation. What they are to-day, such have they ever been; what to-day they know, they have known from the beginning of the world. If born so lavishly endowed, it is because they are incapable of improvement. They live not by their own will, but by the impulse imparted to them by nature. From the creation until now, the beaver has constructed his lodge upon the same plan; the caterpillar and spider woven their cocoons and tissues of the same form; the bee projected his cell of the same hexagon; the lion-ant traced, without a compass, its circles and arches. The character of *their* labours is that of exactitude and uniformity; that of man, diversity,—for

human labour arises from a free and creative faculty of mind.
Judge therefore between them!—Of all created beings, man
alone possesses the idea of duty, of responsibility, of contemplation, of piety. Alone of all the earth he is endowed with insight
into futurity, and the knowledge of life and death."

"But is this knowledge an advantage? is it a source of happiness?" demanded the Count. "Why has GOD bestowed upon us
reason by which we are led astray, and learning which serves but
to perplex us? With all our superiority, how often are we forced
to despise ourselves!—Why is the exclusively privileged being
the only one liable to error? Is not the instinct of animals preferable to *our* glimmering reason?"

"Both species were not created for the same end. GOD requires not virtue of the brute creation. Were *they* endowed with
reason, with liberty of choice as regards their food and lodgment,
the equilibrium of the world would be destroyed. The will of
the Creator decided that the surface of the globe, and even its
depths, should be filled with animated beings,—that life should
pervade the universe; in pursuance of which, plains, valleys,
forests, from the mountain top to the lowest chasms,—trees, rocks,
rivers, lakes, oceans, from the sandy desert to the marshy swamp,
—in all climates and latitudes,—from one pole to the other,—all
is peopled,—all instinct with life, all blended in one vast sphere
of existence. Whether sheltered in the depths of the wilderness,
or behind a blade of grass, the lion and the pismire are alike at
the post assigned them by nature. Each has his part to play, his
place to guard, his predestined line of action; each is enchained
within his proper bound; for every square of the infinite chessboard was from the first appropriately filled. Man alone is free to
range over all, to traverse oceans and deserts;—pitch his tent on
the sand, or construct a floating palace on the waters; to defy the
Alpine snows or the fervours of the torrid zone:—

" ' The world is all before him, where to choose
His place of rest, and Providence his guide ' "

"But if Providence indeed exert such influence, from whence
the crimes arising in all human communities, and the disasters
which overwhelm mankind?" cried Charney. "I sympathize in
your admiration of all created things; my reason is overwhelmed
when I examine the mighty whole, but on descending to the history of the human species—"

"My friend," interrupted Girardi, "arraign not the wisdom of
the Almighty because of the errors of mankind, the devastations
of a hurricane, or the eruptions of a volcano! Immutable laws
are imprinted upon matter; and the work of ages is accomplished,
whether a vessel founder in a storm, or a city disappear beneath

the surface of the earth. Of what account in the sight of the Almighty a few human existences more or less? Does the Supreme Being believe in the reality of death, the darkness of the grave?

"No! But HE has conferred on our souls the power of self government, and this is proved by the independence of our passions. I have portrayed animals submitted to the irresistible influence of instinct, — possessing only blind tendencies, and the qualities inherent in their several species. Man alone is the parent of his virtues and his vices; man alone is endowed with free agency; because for him this earth is a place of probation. The tree of good and evil which we cultivate here, is to bear its fruits in a higher or a lower region. Do you imagine the omniscient GOD so unjust as to leave the afflictions of the virtuous unrewarded? Were this world the limit of our reward and punishment, the man who dies by a stroke of lightning ought to be accounted a malefactor, and the fortune of the prosperous should suffice as a certification of excellence!"

Charney listened in silence: impressed by the simple eloquence of his instructor, his eyes were fixed upon the noble countenance on which the excitement of a mind innately pious was imprinting an almost august character of inspiration.

"But why," at length murmured the Count, "why has not GOD vouchsafed us the positive certainty of our immortality?"

"Doubt was perhaps indispensable," replied the venerable man, rising and placing his hand affectionately on the shoulder of his youthful companion, "to repress the vanity of human reason. What is the merit of virtue, if its rewards be assured beforehand? What would become of free will? The soul of man is expansive, but not infinite;—vast in its power of apprehending its own distinctions, and of appreciating the Creator by the mightiness of his works; yet so limited as to render it profoundly sensible of its dependence upon Providence. Man is permitted a glimpse of his destinies—FAITH must effect the rest.

"Oh! mighty and all-seeing God!" cried Girardi, —suddenly interrupting himself, and clasping his hands in all the fervour of supplication, "lend me the strength of thine arm to upraise from the dust this man who is struggling with his human weakness and the desire to reach thy fountains of light! Lend me thy wisdom to direct the aspirations of this longing and bewildered soul! Lend eloquence to the words of my lips, that they may be endued with the strength and power of the faith that is in me! The humblest of thy creations—a flower, and an insect—have startled the sceptic in his self-security; give grace to these, O Lord! if not to me, to perfect the work thine infinite mercy has begun; and if not by me, by the humble plant before us, be the miracle of thy holiness accomplished!"

The old man was silent. An ecstacy of prayer had taken possession of his soul; and when, at the close of his unuttered devotions, he turned towards his companion, Charney was bending his head upon his hands, clasped together upon the back of the bench where they were sitting. On raising his head, his countenance bore traces of the most devout meditation.

CHAPTER VIII.

In the purified heart of Charney, the blood now flowed more calmly: in his expanded mind, mild and consolatory ideas succeeded each other in gentle gradation. Like the wise Piedmontese, his friend, he was fully alive to the conviction that happiness connects itself indissolubly with love of our fellow-creatures; and in striving to people his imagination with those to whom he was bound by ties of gratitude; the Empress, Girardi, and Ludovico, presented themselves first to his mind. But at length, two female shadows became perceptible at either extremity of this rainbow of love, expanding after the storm, just as we see in altar-pieces, two seraphim, with brows inclined, and half-closed wings, supporting the arch of the picture.

One of these shadows was the fairy of his dreams,—the maiden Picciola, emanating, fresh, fair, and blooming, from the perfumes of his flower; the other, the guardian angel of his prison, — his second providence,—Teresa Girardi.

By a singular inconsistency, the former, whose existence was purely ideal, haunted his memory in a fixed, distinct, and positive form; he could discern the varying expression of her brow, the glittering of her eye, the smile of her lips;—such as she had once appeared to him in his dreams, such was she ever manifested. Whereas Teresa, on whom he had never fixed his eyes, or only while still under the influence of a waking dream, under what traits could he summon her to his remembrance? In *her* instance, the countenance of the seraph was veiled; and when Charney, in despair, attempted to raise the veil, it was still the face of Picciola that smiled upon him: of Picciola, multiplying herself as if for the purpose of interrupting the homage he would fain have offered to her rival.

One morning, the prisoner of Fenestrella, though wide awake, fancied himself alarmingly deminated by this strange hallucination. The day was dawning. Having risen from his cheerless bed, he was musing upon Girardi, who, prepared for his speedy release from prison, had infused such tenderness into his adieu of the preceding night, that the Count had been kept all night sleepless by the impression of their approaching separation. After pacing his room for some time in silence, he looked out from his grated window upon the bench of conference, where, only the evening before, he had been engaged with Girardi in conversation relative to his daughter; and lo! through the gray-hued mists of autumn, he fancied he could discern a woman,—the figure of a young and graceful woman,—seated on the spot. She was alone, and in an inclining attitude; as if engaged in contemplation of the flower before her.

Recalling to mind the probability of Teresa's arrival, Charney naturally exclaimed—"It is herself! Teresa is arrived! I am about to see her for a moment, and then behold her face no more; and in losing her, I shall also be deprived of my venerated companion."

As he spoke, the figure turned towards his window; and the countenance revealed to him by the movement was no other than the face of his dream-love — of Picciola, — still and always, Picciola!

Stupified by the discovery, he passed his hand over his brow, his eyes, his garments, the cold iron bars of his window—in order to be satisfied that he was awake, and that *this* time, at least, it was not a dream.

The young woman rose, moved a few paces towards him, and smiling and blushing, addressed him a confused gesture of salutation; but Charney made no acknowledgment, either of the smile or the gesture by which it was accompanied. He kept his eye fixed upon the graceful form which traversed the misty court; a form in every point resembling that with which his ideal Picciola was invested in the dreams of his solitude. Fancying himself under the influence of delirium, he threw himself on the bed, in hopes of recovering his composure and presence of mind. Some minutes afterwards, the door opened, and Ludovico made his appearance.

"*Oimé! oimé!*—Sad news and great news, *eccellenza!*" cried he. "One of my birds is about to take flight—not over the walls, indeed, but over the drawbridge. So much the better for him, and the worse for you."

"Is it to be to-day, then?" demanded Charney, in a tone of emotion.

"I hardly know, *Signor Conte;* but it can't be far off; for the act of release has been already signed in Paris, and is known to be on its way to Turin; at least, so the young lady just now told her father in my hearing."

"How!" cried Charney, starting from his reclining attitude. "She is arrived, then—she is *here!*"

"At Fenestrella, *eccellenza*, since yesterday evening, and provided with a formal order for her admission into the fortress. But there is a special injunction against letting down the drawbridge after hours, for a female; so she was obliged to put off her visit till this morning, *Capo di Dio!* I knew she was there, but kept the secret as close as wax. Not a syllable did I let fall before the poor old gentleman, or he would not have had a wink of sleep. The night would have seemed as long as ten, had he known that his child was so near. This morning she was up before the sun; and waited for admittance at the gates of the citadel, in the morning fogs,—like a good soul and good daughter, as she is."

"And did she not wait some time in the courtyard,—seated yonder on the bench?" cried Charney, confounded by all he was hearing. And, rushing to the window, he cast an inquiring glance anew upon the little court, adding, in an altered voice, "But she is gone, I see! she is there no longer!"

"Of course not,—*now;* but she *was* there half an hour ago," replied the gaoler. "She stayed in the court while I went up stairs to prepare her father for the visit; for the poor young lady had heard that people may die of joy. Joy, you see, *excellenza*, is like spirituous liquors;—a thimblefull, now and then, does a man a power of good; but, let him toss off a whole gourd, and there's an end of him at once. Now, bless their poor hearts, they are together; and, seeing them so happy, *per Bacco*, I found myself suddenly all of a no-how; which made me think of your excellency, and how you were about to be deprived of your friend; and so I made off to remind you that Ludovico will still be left you,—to say nothing of Picciola. To be sure, poor thing, she is losing her beauty;—scarce a leaf left. But *that* is the natural effect of the season. You must not despise her for *that*."

And the gaoler quitted the room, without waiting the reply of Charney; who, deeply affected, vainly tried to explain to himself the mysteries of his vision. He was now almost persuaded that the sweet figure by which his dreams were haunted, to which he had assigned the name of Picciola, was the creature of reminiscence;—that, absorbed by interest in his plant, he had cast his eyes on Teresa Girardi, as she stood at the grated window, and unwittingly received an impression eventually reproduced by his dreams.

While he was thus reasoning, the murmur of two voices reached him from the stairs; and, in addition to the well-known steps of the old man, gliding over the stones, he could distinguish the light, airy foot of one who scarcely seemed to touch the steps as she descended. At length, the measured sound ceased at his door. He started. But Girardi made his appearance alone.

"My daughter is here," said the old man. "She is waiting for us beside your plant."

Charney followed in silence. He had not courage to articulate a syllable. A consciousness of pain and constraint chased every feeling of pleasure from his heart.

Was this the consequence of being about to present himself before a woman to whom he was so largely indebted, and towards whom it was impossible for him to discharge the obligation; or of shame for his ungraciousness of the morning, in neglecting to return her smile and salutation? As the time of separation from Girardi approached, were his fortitude and resignation forsaking him? No matter what the motive of his embarrassment in presenting himself before Teresa Girardi, no one could have discerned, in his language or demeanour, traces of the brilliant and popular Count de Charney:—the ease of the man of the world, the self-possession of the philosopher, had given place to an awkwardness, a hesitation, which called forth, in the answers of Teresa, a correspondent tone of coldness and circumspection.

In spite of all Girardi's exertions to place his daughter and his friend on an agreeable footing, their conversation turned only upon indifferent subjects, or trite remarks upon the dawning hopes of all parties. Having in some degree recovered from his emotion, Charney read, in the features of the lovely Piedmontese, only the most complete indifference; and persuaded himself that the services she had rendered him had been instigated by the impulses of a generous disposition; or, perhaps, by the commands of her father.

Charney began almost to regret that the interview had taken place; for he felt that he could never more invest her, in his reveries, with her former fascinations. While all three were seated on the bench, Girardi, wrapt in contemplation of his daughter, and Charney giving utterance to a few cold, incoherent remarks, there escaped, from the folds of Teresa's dress, as she was drawn suddenly forward, by the tender embrace of her father, a medallion of gold and crystal. On stooping to pick it up, Charney could readily discern that one side was occupied by a lock of her father's gray hair; and the other by a withered flower. He looked again; he gazed anxiously; he could not mistake it. The hidden treasure was the identical flower of Picciola which he had sent her by Ludovico.

Teresa had kept his flower, then—had preserved it—treasured it with the gray hairs of her father—the father whom she adored! The flower of Picciola no longer adorned the raven tresses of the young girl, but rested upon her heart! This discovery produced an instantaneous revolution in the sentiments of Charney. He began to reconsider the charms of Teresa, as if a new personage had offered herself to his observation—as if he had seen her metamorphosed by enchantment before his eyes.

The Count now perceived that, as she turned her expressive looks towards her father, the two-fold character of tenderness and placidity impressed upon her beauty, was analogous with that of Raphael's Madonnas;—that she was lovely with the loveliness of a pure and perfect soul. Charney retraced, with deliberate admiration, her animated profile—her countenance, expressive of the union of strength and softness, energy and timidity. It was long since he had looked upon a new human face;—how much longer since he had contemplated, in combination, youth, beauty, and virtue! The spectacle seemed to intoxicate his senses; and, after a glance at the graceful form and perfect symmetry of Teresa Girardi, his wandering eyes fixed themselves once more on the medallion.

"You did not disdain my humble offering, then!" faltered the Count; and faint as was the whisper in which the words were conveyed, they roused the pride of Teresa; who, advancing her hand to receive the trinket, replaced it hurriedly in her dress. But at that moment she was struck by the change of expression visible in the features of the Count; and both their faces became suffused with blushes.

"What is the matter, my dear child?" demanded Girardi, noticing her confusion.

"Nothing!" she replied, with emotion. Then, as if ashamed of playing the hypocrite with her parent, suddenly added, "This medallion, father, contains a lock of your hair." Then, as she turned towards Charney,—"And this flower, sir, is the one you sent me by Ludovico. I have preserved it, and shall keep it forever."

In her words,—in the sound of her voice,—in the intuitive modesty which induced her to unite her father and the stranger in her explanations, there was at once so much ingenuousness and purity of feminine instinct, that Charney began for the first time to appreciate the true merits of Teresa Girardi.

The remainder of that happy day elapsed amid effusions of mutual friendship, which every moment seemed to enhance. Independent of the secret power which attracts us towards another, the progress of friendship is always rapid in proportion to the time we know to be allowed us for the cultivation of dawning partiality. This was the first day that Charney and Teresa had conversed together; but they had had occasion to think so much of each other, and so few hours were assigned them to be together, that a mutual acquaintance was speedily accomplished; so that, when Charney, impelled by good breeding and good feeling, would fain have retired, in order to afford an opportunity to the father and daughter, so long separated, to converse together alone, Girardi and Teresa alike opposed the movement of retreat.

"Are you about to leave us!" said the latter. "Do you, then, consider yourself a stranger to my father, *or to me?*" added the young girl in a tone of gentle reproach. And, in order to make him fully apprehend how little restraint was imposed upon her by his presence, Teresa began to detail to her father all that had befallen her from the moment of her departure from Fenestrella, and the means she had employed to bring together the two captives; addressing, at the conclusion of her narrative, a request to Charney, to relate all the little events of the citadel, and the progress of his studies connected with Picciola. After this appeal, the Count did not hesitate to confess the history of his early miseries,—the tedium of his captivity,—and the blessing vouchsafed him in the arrival of his plant: while Teresa, gay and naïve, stimulated his confession, by the liveliness of her inquiries and repartees.

Seated between the two, and holding a hand of each,—of the daughter thus restored to him, and the friend he was about to leave,—the venerable Girardi listened to their discourse with an air of mingled joy and sadness. At one moment, when, by a spontaneous movement, he was about to clasp his hands, thos of Charney and Teresa were brought almost into contact, the two young people appeared startled, touched, embarrassed, and, though silent, communicated their emotion to each other by a rapid glance. But, without affectation or prudery, Teresa soon disengaged her hand from that of her father; and, placing it affectionately on his shoulder, looked smilingly towards the Count, as if inviting him to resume his narrative.

Enchanted and emboldened by so much grace and candour, Charney described the reveries produced by the emanations of his plant. How could he forbear allusion to that which constituted the great event of his captivity? He spoke of the fair being whom he had been induced to worship as the personification of Picciola; and, while tracing her portrait with warmth,—or rather transport,—the smiles of Teresa gradually disappeared, and her bosom swelled with agitation.

The narrator was careful to assign no name to the soft image he tried to call up before their eyes; but when, in completing the history of the disasters of his plant, he reached the moment when, by order of the commandant, the dying Picciola was on the eve of being torn up before his eyes, Teresa could not refrain from a cry of sympathy.

"My poor Picciola!" cried she.

"*Thine!*" reiterated her father, with a smile.

"Yes, *mine!* Did I not contribute to her preservation?" persisted Teresa.

And Charney, in confirming her title to the adoption, felt as if, from that moment, a sacred bond of community were established between them for evermore.

CHAPTER IX.

GLADLY would the Count de Charney have renounced his liberty for the remainder of his days, could he have secured the sentence of passing them at Fenestrella, between Teresa Girardi and her father. He no longer deceived himself. He felt that he loved Teresa as he had never loved before. A sentiment to which his breast had hitherto been a stranger, now penetrated into its depths, impetuous and gentle, sweet and stimulating, like some acid fruit of the tropics, at once sweet and refreshing. His new passion revealed itself not only by transports hitherto unknown, but by the serene glow of a holy tenderness, embracing universal nature; nay, the great Lord and Creator of nature and nature's works.

His brain, his heart, his whole existence, seemed to dilate, as if to embrace the new hopes, projects, and emotions, crowding on his regenerate existence.

Next day, the three friends met again beside Picciola; Girardi and the Count occupying their bench, and Teresa a chair of state, placed opposite them by the gallantry of Ludovico. She had brought with her some task of woman's work, some strip of delicate embroidery, over which her soft countenance inclined, her graceful head following the movements of her needle; and every now and then raising her eyes and suspending her work, to interpose some playful remark in their grave dissertations. At length suddenly rising, she crossed over towards her father, threw her arms round his neck, and pressed her lips repeatedly to his reverend locks.

The conversation between the two disputants was not renewed: for Charney was already absorbed in profound meditation. He could not forbear inquiring of himself whether he were beloved in return by Teresa!—a question which produced two conflicting sentiments in his bosom. He feared to believe—he trembled to doubt. The flower—his gift—so carefully preserved,—the emotion evinced when their hands were accidentally united on the knees of the old man,—the tremor with which she had listened to the recital of his impassioned dreams,—all this was in his favour. But the words breathed with so tender an inflexion of voice had been pronounced in the presence of her father; what sense, therefore, dared he assign to her tokens of compassion, her deeds of kindness and devotion? Had she not afforded proofs of the same good-will before they had even met—before even an interchange of looks and words had taken place between them? What right has he to interpret in his favour, the indications of feeling he has since detected in her deportment?

No matter: of his own attachment, at least, he is certain. *He* not only loves Teresa, but has sworn within his heart of hearts to love her through life and death; substituting for an ideal image, henceforward superfluous, one of the most charming realities of human nature.

But the attachment of which he is thus conscious is a secret to be preserved in the inmost archives of his soul: it would be a sin, a crime, to invoke the participation of Teresa in his passion. What right has he to imbitter the happy prospects of *her* life? Are they not destined to live apart from each other? *she*, free, happy, in the midst of a world which she embellishes, and where she will doubtless soon confer happiness on another in the bosom of domestic life; while *he*, in his solitary prison, must consecrate himself to eternal solitude and eternal regrets for his momentary happiness

No! his passion shall be sedulously concealed. He will assume towards Teresa Girardi the demeanour of a person wholly indifferent, or satisfy himself with the calm demonstrations of a prudent and equable friendship. It would be too deep a misfortune for *him*—for *both*—were he to succeed in engaging her affections.

Full of these fine projects for the future, the first sounds that meet his ear on the cessation of his reverie, were the following sentences interchanged between Teresa and her father, the former of whom was exerting all her eloquence to persuade the old man that the moment of his liberation was at hand; while Girardi persisted in expressing a conviction that the remainder of the year would expire without producing any material change in his destinies. "I know the dilatoriness of public functionaries," said he; "I know the vacillations of government. So little suffices as a pretext for the suspension of justice, and the cooling of a great man's mercy!"

"If such is your opinion," cried Teresa, "I will return to-morrow to Turin, to hasten the fulfilment of their promises."

"What need of so much haste?" demanded her father.

"How, dear father!" she replied, "is it possible that you prefer your mean and narrow chamber, and this wretched court, to your beautiful villa and gardens on the Collina?"

This seeming anxiety on the part of Teresa to leave Fenestrella ought to have convinced Charney that he was beloved, and that the danger that he dreaded for the object of his romantic attachment was already consummated. But the part he had intended to play was now wholly frustrated. Instead of affecting indifference, tranquillity, or even the reserve of a prudent friendship, he manifested only the petulance of a lover. Teresa, however, remained apparently unconscious of his fit of perversity; and was not deterred by his resentment from repeating, that if the decree of her father's liberation should be again delayed, it was her duty to set off for Turin, and renew her solicitations to General Menon; nay, even for Paris, for a personal application to the Emperor. Usually so reserved and mild, the fair Piedmontese seemed excited on the present occasion to unusual vivacity.

"I scarcely understand you this morning," said her father, amazed to observe the gaiety of her deportment in presence of the poor prisoner whom they were about to abandon to his misfortunes; and if her father found something to regret in her demeanour, how much rather the grieved and disappointed Charney!

The same reflections which had perplexed his mind the preceding night had, in fact, been passing also through the mind of Teresa. She had discovered, *not* the arrival of Love in her bosom, but that it had long resided there an unsuspected inmate·

and though, like Charney, she would willingly have accepted, as regarded her own happiness, the perils and privations with which it was accompanied, like Charney she was reluctant that all these should be inflicted upon another. The delight of loving, the dread of being loved, threw her into a state of mental contradiction, and produced the garrulity in which she sought refuge from herself.

Soon, however, all this constraint, all these efforts to disguise their real sentiments, were suddenly dropped on both sides. After listening attentively to the information imparted by Girardi, who mentioned frequent instances where the pardon of prisoners, though publicly announced, had not been suffered to take effect for many succeeding months, the young people allowed themselves to be convinced; and with mutual and unconcealed delight, began forming projects for the morrow and succeeding days, as if, henceforward, the fortress of Fenestrella were to be the home of their happiness and choice. Restored to the society of Teresa, their guardian angel, the two captives appeared to have but a single earthly misfortune to apprehend, the liberation of one of them to disunite the little party.

Already, the philosophers were resuming their arguments, and Teresa her embroidery. The pale rays of the sun, partially illuminating the little court, fell lightly on the countenance of Girardi's daughter, while a refreshing breeze played amid the folds of her drapery and the floating ribands by which it was confined. At length, excited by the freshness of the atmosphere, she threw aside her work, rose from her seat, shook out the ringlets of her raven hair, rejoicing in the return of hope and sunshine, when suddenly the postern-door was thrown open, and Captain Morand, accompanied by Ludovico and a municipal officer, made his appearance.

They came to signify to Giacomo Girardi the act of his enlargement. He was to quit Fenestrella without delay; a carriage was in waiting at the extremity of the glacis to convey him and his daughter to Turin.

At the moment of the commandant's arrival, Teresa was standing beside her father, but she instantly sank backward in her chair, resumed her needlework, and, had Charney ventured a look towards her, he would have been startled, on perceiving how instantaneously the hues of life and health had faded from her cheek. But Charney neither stirred nor raised his eyes from the ground, while Girardi was receiving from the hands of the officers those papers and documents which were to restore him, with an unblemished reputation, to his station in society. All was now complete; and there was no longer an excuse for prolonging the liberated prisoner's preparations for departure.

Ludovico had already brought down from Girardi's chamber
13*

the solitary trunk containing his effects;—the officers waited to escort him back to Turin;—the hour of parting had irrevocably struck. Rising once from her seat, Teresa began deliberately to put up her working materials, and arrange the scarf upon her shoulders; she even tried to put on her gloves, but her hands trembled too much to effect her purpose.

Charney stood for a moment paralysed by the blow. Then arming himself with courage, he exclaimed, as he threw himself into the arms of Girardi—

"Farewell, my dearest father!"

"Farewell, *my son!* farewell, my beloved son," faltered the good old man. "Be of good cheer. Rely upon our exertions in your behalf; rely on the steadiness of our affection. Adieu, adieu!"

For some moments longer Girardi held him pressed to his heart; then, by a sudden effort, relinquishing his warm embrace, turned towards Ludovico, and, by way of concealing his own emotion, affected to busy himself by giving in charge to the gaoler the friend he was about to leave; to which the poor fellow, perfectly comprehending the old man's motives, replied only by offering the support of his arm to conduct his faltering steps to the carriage.

Charney, meanwhile, drew near to Teresa for the purpose of a last farewell. Leaning with one hand on the back of her chair, her eyes fixed on the ground, she stood motionless, speechless, as if there were no question of quitting the place. Even when the Count advanced towards her, she remained for some moments without speaking, till, irresistibly moved by his paleness and agitation, she exclaimed, "I call our Picciola to witness that"— But Teresa was not able to complete the sentence; her heart was too full to utter another syllable. One of her gloves at that moment escaped her trembling hands, which Charney picked up; and, ere he restored it, raised it silently to his lips.

"Keep it!" said she, while tears streamed down her cheeks; "keep it till we meet again."

Another moment, and she was following her father. They were gone! All was dark in the destinies of the Count de Charney. After watching the closing of the postern-door, he stood like one petrified, with his eyes fixed on the spot where they had disappeared; his hand still grasping convulsively the parting pledge bestowed upon him by Teresa.

CONCLUSION.

A PHILOSOPHER has remarked that greatness must be renounced before it can be appreciated; the same thing might have been said of fortune, happiness, or any mode of enjoyment liable to become habitual.

Never had the poor captive of Fenestrella so venerated the wisdom of Girardi, the charms and virtues of his daughter, as after the departure of his two companions! Profound sadness succeeded to this momentary elation. The efforts of Ludovico, the attentions required by Picciola, were unsufficient to divert his attention from his sorrows. But at length, the sources of consolation he had derived from the study of nature brought forth their fruit; and the depressed Charney gradually resumed his strength of mind.

His last stroke of affliction had perfected the happy frame of his feelings. His first impulse had been to bless the loneliness which afforded his whole leisure to muse upon his absent friends; but eventually he learned to behold with satisfaction a new guest seated in the vacant place of the old man.

His first and most assiduous visiter was the chaplain of the prison: even the worthy priest whom during his illness he had so harshly repulsed. Apprised by Ludovico of the state of despair to which the prisoner was reduced, he made his appearance, forgetful of the past, to offer his good offices, which were received with courtesy and gratitude. More amicably disposed than formerly towards mankind, the Count soon became favourably, nay, even affectionately disposed towards the man of God; and the rustic seat became once more the bench of conference. The philosopher loved to enlarge upon the wonders of his plant, the wonders of nature, and repeat the lessons of the excellent Girardi; while the priest, without bringing forward a single dogma of religion, contented himself, in the first instance, with reciting the sublime moral lessons of Christianity: grounding their strength upon the principles already imbibed by the votary of natural religion.

The second visiter was the commandant; and Charney now discovered that Morand was essentially a good sort of man, whose heart was militarily disciplined; that is, disposed to torment the unfortunate beings under his charge no farther than he was necessitated by the letter of government instructions. So just, too, did he show himself in his appreciation of the merits of the two prisoners recently released, as almost to put Charney into good humour with petty tyranny.

But all this was soon to end; and it became Charney's turn to bid adieu to the priest and the captain. One fine day, when least prepared for the concession, the gates of his prison opened, and he was set at liberty!

On Napoleon's return from Austerlitz, incessantly importuned by Josephine, (who had probably some person besetting her in turn with supplications in favour of the prisoner of Fenestrella,) the Emperor caused an inquiry to be made into the nature of the papers seized among the effects of the Count de Charney. The cambric manuscripts were accordingly forwarded to the Tuileries, from the archives of the police, where they had been deposited; and, attracted by the singularity of their appearance, Napoleon himself deigned to investigate the indications of treason contained in their mysterious records.

"The Count de Charney is a madman," exclaimed the Emperor, after most deliberate examination; "a visionary and a madman; but not the dangerous person represented to me. He who could submit his powers of mind to the influence of a sorry weed, may have in him the making of an excellent botanist, but not of a conspirator. He is pardoned! Let his estates be restored to him, that he may cultivate there, unmolested, his own fields, and his taste for natural history."

Need it be added that the Count did not loiter at Fenestrella after receiving this welcome intelligence; or that he did not quit the fortress alone? but, transplanted into a solid case, filled with good earth, Picciola made her triumphal exit from her gloomy birthplace;—Picciola, to whom he owed his life—nay, more than life,—his insight into the wondrous works of God, and the joys resulting from peace and good-will towards mankind;—Picciola, by whom he has been betrayed into the toils of love;—Picciola, through whose influence, finally, he is released from bondage!

As Charney was about to cross the drawbridge of the citadel, a rude hand was suddenly extended towards him. "*Eccellenza!*" said Ludovico, repressing his rising emotion, "give us your hand! we may be friends now that you are going away;—now that you are about to leave us;—now that we shall see your face no more! —Thank Heaven, we may now be friends!"

Charney heartily embraced him. "We *shall* meet again, my good Ludovico," cried he; "I promise you that you do not see me for the last time." And, having shaken both the hands of the gaoler again and again with the utmost cordiality, the Count quitted the fortress.

After his carriage had traversed the esplanade, and left far behind the mountain on which the citadel is situated, crossed the bridge over the Clusone, and attained the Suza road, a voice still continued crying aloud from the ramparts — "*Addio, Signor Conte! Addio, addio, Picciola!*"

* * * * * * * * * * *

Six months afterwards, a rich equipage stopped at the gate of the state prison of Fenestrella; from which alighted a traveller inquiring for Ludovico Ritti: the former prisoner was come to pay a visit to his gaoler! A young lady, richly attired, was leaning tenderly upon his arm,—Teresa Girardi, now Countess de Charney. Together, the young couple visited the little court, and the miserable camera, so long the abode of weariness, scepticism, and despair. Of all the sentences which had formerly disfigured the wall, one only had been suffered to remain;—

" Learning, wit, beauty, youth, fortune, are insufficient to confer happiness upon man '

To which the gentle hand of Teresa now added, " if unshared by affection:"—and a kiss, deposited by Charney upon her lovely cheek, seemed to confirm her emendation.

The Count was come to request Ludovico would stand godfather to his first-born child which was to make its appearance before the close of the year: and, the object of their mission accomplished, the young couple proceeded to Turin, where, in his beautiful villa, Girardi was awaiting their return.

There, in a garden closely adjoining his own apartment, in the centre of a rich parterre, warmed and brightened by the beams of the setting sun, Charney had deposited his beloved plant, out of reach of all danger or obstruction. By his especial order, no hand but his own was to minister to her culture. He alone was to watch over Picciola. It was an occupation, a duty, a tax eternally adopted by his gratitude.

How quickly—how enchantingly did his days now glide along! In the midst of exquisite gardens, on the banks of a beautiful stream, under an auspicious sky, Charney was the happiest of the human kind! Time imparted only additional strength to the ties in which he had enchained himself; as the ivy cements and consolidates the wall it embraces. The friendship of Girardi, the tenderness of Teresa, the attachment of all who resided under his roof, conspired to form his happiness, perfected at the happy moment when he heard himself saluted as a father.

Charney's affection for his son soon seemed to rival that he bore his young and lovely wife. He was never weary of contemplating and adoring them; and could scarcely make up his mind to lose sight of them for a moment. And lo! when Ludovico Ritti arrived from Fenestrella, to fulfil his promise to the Count, and proceeded to visit, in the first instance, his original goddaughter,—the god-daughter of the prison,—he found that, amid all this domestic happiness,—all these transports of joy and affection,—all the rapture and prosperity brightening the home of the Count and Countess de Charney, PICCIOLA had been forgotten:—*La povera Picciola* had died of neglect, unnoticed and unlamented. The appointed task was over. The herb of grace had nothing farther to unfold to the happy husband, father, and believer!

THE END.

www.ingramcontent.com/pod-product-compliance
Lightning Source LLC
Chambersburg PA
CBHW031459160426
43195CB00010BB/1029